PRAISE FOR FAY JACOBS' BOOKS

"Her columns . . . are laugh out loud funny and the best part is that Jacobs is sincere . . . Those who enjoyed Jacobs' (other collections) will not be disappointed and those reading her for the first time will understand why she's such a beloved columnist."
—Jane van Ingen, *Lambda Book Report*

"It's an intelligent, hysterically funny, and occasionally poignant look at how we live today, with hopes for tomorrow. Recommended for everyone, male or female, gay or straight. Five stars out of five."
—*Echo Magazine*

"She makes you laugh, and she makes you think—and then you laugh again and again and again."
—Comedienne Jennie McNulty

"Fay Jacobs is not just a treasure to the peoples of Rehoboth Beach and Delaware, she's a national treasure for *all* of us."
—Publisher Salem West

"Every bit as sardonic, witty, sarcastic, and insightful as her other books!"
—Richard LaBonte, *San Francisco Bay Times*

"Fay Jacobs' hilarious dispatches are funny, touching—and real. This is a true laugh riot, as Fay wittily takes on sexuality, politics, relationships, and day-to-day dilemmas."
—*Insight Out Book Club*

"Every tale is masterfully told—these memorable memoirs . . . are both pleasure and treasure."
—Anna Furtado, *Just About Write*

"Fay's writing is everything we've come to expect—humorous, insightful, and savvy. Fay finds universal messages in everyday experiences, entertaining while reminding us of all that binds us together. Laugh, cry, and above all, rejoice with Fay Jacobs' newest collection."

—Author and publisher, Radclyffe

"Fay Jacobs' sharp wit turns frustrating everyday events into laugh-out-loud medicine worthy of award-winning stand-up comedy. My sides hurt long after reading, but I still beg for more. Keep writing!"

—Author Carsen Taite

"Pure Borscht Belt gold—a funny, wisely observed & politically astute read."

—*Out in Print*

Fay Jacobs' Rehoboth Beach Diaries

As I Lay Frying
Fried & True
For Frying Out Loud
Time Fries
Fried & Convicted

BIG GIRLS DON'T FRY

REHOBOTH BEACH WRAP UP

FAY JACOBS

2024

Bywater Books

Copyright © 2024 Fay Jacobs

All rights reserved. No part of this book may be reproduced, stored in a retrieval system, or transmitted in any form or by any means, without prior permission in writing from the publisher.

Print ISBN: 978-1-61294-289-6

Bywater Books First Edition: April 2024

Printed in the United States of America on acid-free paper.

Cover design: TreeHouse Studio

Bywater Books
PO Box 3671
Ann Arbor MI 48106-3671

www.bywaterbooks.com

This is a memoir in columns. The events, places, and conversations are portrayed to the best of the author's memory. While all the stories in this book are true, the chronology of some events has been compressed. When necessary, the names and identifying characteristics of individuals, Schnauzers, and places have been changed to maintain anonymity.

Dedication

To my wife Bonnie, and the preservation of democracy.

TABLE OF CONTENTS

Foreword by Eric C. Peterson

Prologue

2017
Women (and Men) Take to the Streets	3
It's a Windfall Inheritance	7
Hoofstock	10
The Accidental Publisher	13
Celebrating Family	19
Travel Bingo: Everything Old Is New Again	22
Ready, Set, Gurgitate!	25
Applying Myself	28
Aging Gracelessly, All Ears	31
Not Down in the Dumps	35
Out the Windows into Cyberspace	39
Infotainment!	42

2018
Cyclone Snow Bomb 1, Yeti 0	45
Good Moose Hunting	48
For Steve Elkins	51
Back in the Saddle Again	56
For the Love of Stuff	58
Not a Spitting Chance	61
It's Pride Month and I'm Feeling It	64
Slots of Fun	67
Drinks Well with Others	70
Ooh La La!	73
Avez Vous Any Ice?	76

The Final Straw	79
I Flew at iFLY	82
Press 3 for a Nervous Breakdown	85
On My Honor, I was Shocked	88
When in Rome	92

2019

Am I Queer?	95
Ah Yes I Remember it Well	98
Snowbird Disaster	101
Um, Stuff Happens	104
Young, Scrappy, and Hungry	107
The Human-Animal Bond	110
Damn Spam	113
Hell No, We Won't Go!	116
What Do You Meme I'm Old?	119
The Kids Are All Right	122
A Weekend of Firsts	125
Don't Cry for Me, Marie Kondo	128
I Have Reservations	131
No Place Like It	134
Days of Wine and Roses	137
One of these Days, Alice	139
You Gotta Have Heart	142
Wazy Lazy Days	145
Funny About That…	148

2020

Monster Land Yacht	151
At Least it's Not Corona	154
Pandemic Diary	157
Vanity Fare	161
Out in the Fresh Air	164
Truth Unmasked	167

Pride in June, Pride Year-Round	169
Demolished: A Wild Gay History	174
Home in the Time of Covid	177
Check the Spaghetti Model	180
Thanks for the Memories	183
I Kissed a Penguin	186
Hello, I'm Calling from the IRS	189
Cyber-Bullied	192
Out of the Closet	195
The Margin of Error	198
Bye Bye 2020. I Need a Drink.	201

2021

January 6th, Specifically	204
It's a Real %&^# Show	205
It's Officially Poodle Beach	208
First Plague, Then Pestilence?	211
No Police in Parade? Shame!	214
Let's Get Physical	217
Curtain Up, Cue the Schnauzer	219

2022

It's How I Roll	222
The Game of Crones	225
Grocery Store Hunger Games	228
Make Sure Your Bladder Is Full	231
Postcards from the Edge of the Canyon	234
Sex, Lies, and Video Hate	237

2023

My Dance with Covid (Or Farewell to 2022)	240
The Writer's Life	243
Paddling Against the Tide	246
Juiced Up and Ready to Roll	249

What Price Loyalty	252
Reflections from Kodak	255
Enjoy Yourself	257
Civility Lives!	260
Downhill from Here	263
Get Off My Lawn	265
A Trivial Pursuit	268
Size Matters	271
Epilogue	274

Acknowledgments

About the Author

About Bywater Books

FOREWORD

I was there, a quarter century ago, on a chilly evening in the Rehoboth Art League—when we started brainstorming titles for Fay Jacobs's first book. She wanted it to be memorable, of course, If it suggested the journey of a couple of lesbians from the suburbs discovering the joys of a small, gay-friendly beach town, that would be great. But mostly, she wanted something funny. I suggested that puns are funnier when you take something deadly serious and—by changing one word—create something ridiculous. I can't remember which one of us came up with *As I Lay Frying*, but as soon as we heard it, we all knew it was the one.

And from there, the hits just kept coming: *For Frying Out Loud*, *Fried & True*, *Time Fries*, and *Fried & Convicted*—each packed with Fay's signature blend of wry observations and laugh-out-loud turns of phrase. The volume you hold in your hand represents the final book of the series (although I still hold out hope for a travel memoir called *Fry Away with Me*). And after reading it, what strikes me is the same thing I've always felt about Fay's work—but even more so, this time: how each essay functions as a momentary delight, and how taken together (either as a book, or a series of six books) you begin to feel the weight of history. A rainbow-hued queer history, to be sure, but weighty all the same. It's like the old riddle: How much does a ton of feathers weigh?

    This volume kicks off in 2017, just after the inauguration of one Donald J. Trump. Fay says it was a terrible time to be a humorist, but what I believe is that at no time in my life did I need to laugh as much as I did during the reign of the Mango Mussolini—and Fay delivered on that score. Most of the essays here aren't overtly political. There are other stories, like the one about the time she mailed her saliva to a lab to find out if she was made of anything else but Eastern European bagel bakers. There's a tale about the time she traveled (I remember travel) to Paris for the Gay Games, and another about climbing Mount Blanc in inappropriate footwear. And there are tales of quarantining at home, learning how to FaceTime in lieu of dinner and cocktails with friends, and contracting a rare respiratory disease—which ought not to be funny, but when the disease is called "Boop," well . . . I won't spoil it, but honestly: only Fay would get a life-threatening illness with built-in jokes.

    But that's Fay. She is the personification of "it's funny because it's true," and she's been making us laugh (and ponder, then laugh again) for more than 25 years.

    Onward!

Eric C. Peterson
Rehoboth Beach, Delaware

PROLOGUE

It's finally here. My sixth and final book in the Frying Series.

In the twenty-four years my wife Bonnie and I have lived at the beach, we've shared our homes with a succession of schnauzers, and been domestic partnered, civil unioned and married, twice, through a variety of paperwork and ceremonies. We've been together over forty years, but Bonnie says it's only twenty because she only listens to me half the time.

I love my wife, my life in Rehoboth, and the privilege of writing about any topic that catches my fancy. I continue to have a blast as a columnist, despite having reached and well-surpassed retirement age.

As of 2015, I've become a performer as well, a sit-down comic touring with my one-woman show *Aging Gracelessly: 50 Shades of Fay*. Who knew I could break into show business at an age when I'd be more likely to break a hip?

And one single principle has guided me along this sometimes bumpy but always interesting road.

My father always said, "Nothing is ever so horrible if you wind up with a good story to tell." And have I got stories. Some are fun, some are distressing, and a lot of them are absolutely infuriating. But they've all been fodder for the storyteller in me.

And frankly, this legacy about taking lemons and turning them into typewritten lemonade was best advice my father ever gave me —especially since the rest from that era tended toward "It wouldn't kill you to wear a dress to your sister's wedding" and "You'll never find a husband if you buy a house with another girl"—although he was right on both counts.

And following my dad's advice, I try to find something worthwhile to take from just about every stupid, annoying, or awful thing that happens.

So here comes my sixth collection of essays, these having been published in the magazines *Letters from CAMP Rehoboth* and *Delaware Beach Life*. I love the topic of passing along our culture—and I am happy to share my take on it with you.

So here come the stories. And the opinions. It's been a rough road since my last book which brought us to the end of 2016. Duck and cover, my friends. I'm letting the ink fly.

BIG GIRLS DON'T FRY
REHOBOTH BEACH WRAP UP

JANUARY 20, 2017

Women (and Men) Take to the Streets

"This is what democracy looks like!"

It sure was. By now you've probably read more than enough about the Women's March on Washington. Yes, it was a visceral and urgent reaction to the election of Donald J. Trump. Yes, it was a magnificent outpouring of bodies and emotions. Here's what you might not know.

First, this was a solidarity march. There was spiritual solidarity on our CAMP bus, with everyone excited and motivated. There was literal solidarity on the DC Metro train, with every inch filled by squashed humans. I may have had an affair with a woman I did not know.

I have been marching since I was twenty in 1968 (Anti-Vietnam War). Then the ERA March in '78, the Pro-Choice March in 1986, LGBT March in '87, '93 and 2000.

This was different. Never, absolutely NEVER have there been so many people on Metro or in the streets, no matter what the official bean counters say. This was the biggest, most crowded protest EVER. So many pink pussy hats!

You couldn't march; you could barely shuffle. You could not cut across the marchers without internal injuries, you could not see the trees for the forest of people; it was a moving mass of clothing, applauding hands, raised fists, and waving signs. A great glob of progressives, oozing forward.

It was so overwhelming it made this old protester cry. And I outed myself as ancient when I told a man, with a child on his shoulders, about the time I sat on my father's shoulders as President Truman rode by in 1952. I was four. Relax. Don't do the math. The answer is 68. When the man looked confused, my co-marcher said, "Truman was president a very, very long time ago." With friends like that, who needs enemies?

We came upon a jumbo TV screen where, if we leaned left (always left!) we could almost see the screen, although there was a streetlight in the middle of our sight line. But I could hear Gloria Steinem (even older than me!) and Ashley Judd (brilliant and on fire!), and all the others.

It was so packed nobody was cold, nobody could move, and there wasn't even room to fall down.

So we listened, then inched forward in a slog-like mass, laughing, clutching our co-walkers to keep together. Only my pal's rainbow hat saved us several times from separation.

My favorites: a twenty-year-old guy with a sweatshirt embroidered with "I'm marching for my grandchildren," and the sign with a Trump photo, saying "You're so vain you probably think this march is about you."

Hundreds of people on a trestle bridge above us chanted, "This is what democracy looks like," and we answered with the same chant as we flowed below.

We'd been told to head back to New Carrollton Metro at three, so our bus could leave for Rehoboth at four. With the still growing crowd I was sure we'd need way more than an hour, so I lobbied to leave at two.

Now, anyone who knows me understands that I am NEVER, ever late. It generally annoys people. If I'm even on time, somebody is already getting ready to call the hospitals.

So I badgered my team, "We should head back now, I mean right now." They sort of agreed, as they saw the insane look in my eyes.

We headed toward the Smithsonian Metro, pushing our way upstream, through the mass of marchers surging our way. After a half hour of fighting the throngs we finally got to the Smithsonian Station, and it was closed due to overcrowding.

So, we turned and battered our way toward the L'Enfant Plaza Metro. On our way we spied another jumbo TV screen.

Omigod! Madonna had shown up! Omigod!

We started jumping up and down to her music like twelve-year-olds at a Jonas Brothers concert. This was the biggest moshiest mosh pit ever.

Continuing to ram against the tide, we finally got to the end of a barely moving line and spent the next forty-five minutes inching toward the metro. We got to the train platform, with less than ten minutes to make it back to our bus on time. Holy crap, I was positively going to be late. I hyperventilated.

"Does this go to New Carrollton?" we screamed, and the consensus was "Yes!" as we were literally sucked onto the train by the moving herd.

Again, the train was so packed I wound up with my head under some gentleman's armpit as he hung on to the bar above and my back lodged against a polite, pierced, and tattooed Millennial who kept me upright. We had paid rapt attention when our bus leader told us New Carrollton was the final train stop so not to worry.

By the time I saw a station named "Benning Road" I screamed. "Oh crap, we're on the wrong train!!! And we're going to be even LATER!!!"

Turns out, we were supposed to change to the Orange Line a few stops back. So, we fought our way off the train at the next stop, ran to the other side of the track, got on going the other way, got off and transferred to get to New Carrollton.

I was having a full-blown meltdown by that time, knowing how late we were and not enjoying my outward-bound aversion therapy tour. All those people on the bus would be waiting for our quartet. I was mortified!

We made it back, a total of one hour late. The gang on the bus applauded our arrival and did not throw things. I did a mea culpa down the aisle to my seat and for anybody that missed it, I am sooo, sooo sorry for being LATE!

So that's my tale. I survived being tardy. I was energized

by the march as I had never been before. And I look at things this way: If I can take five minutes a day, every day, to enter the DIY Network Dream Home contest, I can spend five minutes every day calling legislators and working to protect all of our civil rights.

I still cannot believe I had to march again for this same s*it, different year. But I'll be back if I have to. We *WILL* survive!

FEBRUARY 2017

It's a Windfall Inheritance!

Well, it looks like I'm going to be wealthy. Good thing, because with our new leader in the White House I might want to leave the country. Now I'll be able to run away to a private island, buy a big yacht, and age in place in decadent luxury.

I mean why not. Especially since my good friend Barr Rotimi, Esq, (that's how he addressed me, "Dear Good Friend") just wrote and offered to transfer $11.3 million left to me by his client, a nationality of my country (*that's verbatim*), if I only private message him with my bank routing and account number.

But really, I have a conundrum, because I also got an email from Barrister Richard Alapke, Esq., Attorney at Law. I guess they added the two legal suffixes because they thought I wouldn't know the definition of "barrister." Fooled them.

In fact, I'm so smart, I'm not going to pass up this opportunity. I mean it must have taken some incredible effort for them to find me in little Delaware, all the way from their home office in Coutou, Benin Republic in Africa.

And they're so nice. They apologized for intruding on my privacy with their note, even as they were mourning the death of their largest client, a former director of an African Oil and Gas Company who died tragically in a car accident along with his wife and two children. That's horrible!

It's amazing they took time from the funeral arrangements to let me know I'm their sole beneficiary of $11.5 million, because, get this, I have the same surname! Yes, a catastrophe for my dear Jacobs relatives is a bonanza for me and the barrister who will split the bequest. That's some legal fee.

But here's my ethical dilemma. Should I tell the barrister that Jacobs isn't really my surname at all, but that of a long-ago ex-spouse? What's an heir do?

I was pondering these ethical considerations when I got an email from Dr. Ahmed Kabore, who "suspects that this note might meet you with utmost surprise." Well darn right. That's because he says he got my "contact from searching for a foreign partner from the professional data base found in the internet Yahoo tourist search."

Tourist Search? Is that like Star Search? Seriously? I didn't know I was a professional tourist. Florida Snowbird, yes, but a certified tourist? Though at times I have been called certifiable.

I was, however, comforted by the news that the transaction Dr. Kabore offered up from the Audits and Account manager at the African Development Bank (A.D.B.) in a sum of Ten Million, Five Hundred Thousand American dollars comes to me "risk-free and it will never harm your good reputation in your society because no one can trace the Account." Not a real plus, as my good ship Reputation sailed long ago."

But not to minimize this bequest. After all, Dr. K's client Rudi Harmanto died, along with his entire family, in the Indonesian Tsunami in 2004 and since then the money has been sitting in a "suspense account."

I can see that. It's very suspenseful to figure out how to dispose of the money that for thirteen years has been burning a hole in Africa's pocket.

Hold everything! My good fortune is escalating! I just received a private message on Facebook from Mr. Ly Tay Seng, a personal Accountant/Executive with Foreign Trade Bank of Cambodia (FTB). He told me that it's "with good spirit of heart" he has notified me that a "deceased American client that shares almost the same name as yours died as a result of heart-related condition on March 2005."

And here's a shocking coincidence: "His heart condition was due to the death of the members of his family in the tsunami disaster on the 26 December 2004 in Sumatra, Indonesia, where they all lost all their lives." Might they have lost part of their lives?

Now this is complicated. Poor Mr. Fay or Dr. Jacobs, or Jacobi or Jacobson or whatever is almost the same as my stage name, was quite an accomplished guy. He was a "CEO/textile company owner, businessman, a miner at Kruger mining company in Cambodia, a geologist and consultant to several other mining conglomerate in Cambodia, China, Taiwan, Japan, Indonesia, Pakistan, Vietnam and all in Asia." Yes, even I know those places are in Asia.

The biggest news is that "The amount in this account is currently Nineteen Million Three Hundred and Forty Thousand United States Dollars. I want to present you as a beneficiary. I will use my position and influence in our bank to make they release this money to you for us to share. If i wait for days and i do not hear from you, I shall look for another person."

Good grief. How many days? And is this the best offer? And is there a list of Jacobs's online somewhere? Maybe I could track down my ex and let him know about this bequest so he can finally pay me for those bounced checks from 1976.

Or should I get back to Dr. Ahmed Kabore? It's less money but I'd like to help the good doctor (who by the way is also a lawyer and candlestick-maker) by accepting 40 percent of the money, sending him 50 percent with the final 10 percent being "shared to respectable organizations such as charity and the destitute homes around us in the world."

Wow, I've seen a lot of destitute homes. Mine included. Which reminds me. I haven't made my online entry today in the DIY Network's Dream Home Drawing. I know the odds are very slim that I'll win it, but if I get back to Mr. Ly Tay Seng in time, it will all be a moot point.

I'll be filing my stories from some glorious island in the South Pacific. And sitting on a gold toilet like Mr. Trump. Or is the South Pacific a tsunami zone?

JANUARY 2017

Hoofstock, or Gone Wild in the Green Swamp

As Meryl Streep said in her epic film *Out of Africa*, "I had a ranch in Aff-rica," But who'd think we'd find an African ranch in Florida? No less one where I could ride a camel and feed a giraffe?

This forty-seven-acre working farm and wildlife preserve near Tampa was deep in an area called The Green Swamp. Well, the name gave me the yips, but you know how I love an adventure.

So, we drove to the swamp, crossing Withlacoochie Creek, wondering what the creek would have looked like without lachoochie. And were there other kinds of choochies in the water? Did I hear banjo music from a front porch straight out of *Hoarder TV*?

"Watch where you're driving!" I yelled, as tree moss hung so far over the road, we could be driving through a car wash.

It turned out that the Giraffe Ranch sign was so unobtrusive we drove right past it and had to turn around at George & Gladys's BBQ stand. They advertised Alligator Bites. Lunch or warning? We'll never know.

Meanwhile, back at the ranch (Oh, how I've longed to use that phrase literally!) we joined a small group of visitors listening to naturalists talk about the farm, wetlands, roosting sandhill cranes, and endangered species breeding programs.

The ranch owners had been zoo CEOs, studied endangered species breeding, and been on more than thirty African safaris. They invited us onto a twenty-passenger touring jeep where we roamed the range for close encounters with ostrich, zebra, warthogs (ugly but sweet), two pygmy hippopotamus (hippopotamuses? Hippopotami?) and a prehistoric-looking rhino.

Pointing out their house, it was clear they actually had a home on the range where the deer and the antelope play. To be specific, bongo antelope. This species called an even-toed ungulate, raced across the property (would that be ungulating?), giving our Jeep chase. While it wasn't a migration on the Serengeti, it was pretty darn impressive. The Bongos showcased their spiral horns, which, if one dropped off, as they tend to do, could easily open your Pinot Grigio.

Then, a half a dozen giraffes (even-toed ungulates) walked up to our jeep, bending down, *waaay* down, to accept the offered cabbage leaves from our hands. Does giraffe language have a term for "pain in the neck" and were we tourists described that way? I hoped they had a masseuse back at the barn.

I could only stare at these tallest-of-all yet graceful creatures, licking their big floppy lips, giving us sweet smiles and batting their long, beautiful eyelashes. Glorious!

We stopped by the lake to see the baby hippo, which encouraged me to get my hand out of the bag of cheese doodles I was munching. But the thrill of my day was the camel caravan.

We walked to the Camelot (Could. Not. Resist.), asking the eternal question, "One hump or two?"

My spouse rode a dromedary (one hump) while I was assigned the two-hump model. Both kinds use their humps to store up to eighty pounds of fat for fuel when nourishment is scarce. I was tempted to offer them the cheese doodles, as the fat is better off in a camel's hump than this writer's rump. Just sayin'.

So, there I was, standing on a boardwalk, with a camel parked alongside. They had to give me a footstool, so I could step up, balance on my right leg and throw my left leg over Omar. I will see the physical therapist Tuesday.

I sat, precariously, on a saddle cinched around the belly of the beast. A large grab bar behind the camel's hump provided minimum security as I held on, white knuckled, as we lumbered off. In the last century, before cigarette ads were banned, I might have walked a mile for a camel but now I was unsure if I could survive a mile *on* a camel.

And Omar had me swaying so far from side to side I craved Dramamine.

I thought his fur would be coarse and scratchy, but it was actually soft and fuzzy. Occasionally he turned his head to look at me, his huge eyes inquiring "You okay?"

"Ummm, not sure," I said, "thanks for asking." Meanwhile, Gus, the dromedary behind me, kept trying to pass on the right, whispering sweet nothings in my ear.

The fifteen-minute excursion, past our giraffe friends, past the rhino getting a sponge bath, around the monkey habitat, wasn't exactly an African safari, but it was exhilarating and a really, really cool adventure. And roughly $19,800 dollars cheaper than a National Geo safari. I think we got our money's worth.

At caravan's end, Omar patiently waited for me to dismount ("*Ow, ow, ow!*" that was me, not him.), I thanked him for the lift and gave him a peck on his fuzzy cheek.

As Katy Perry might have sung, I kissed a camel, and I liked it.

FEBRUARY 2017

The Accidental Publisher

Forgive me if you've heard this story before. But I want to reflect on a big change in my status as a publisher and let my readers know.

Back in 2006 I had two cars baking out on the driveway and a garage overflowing with pallets of books. I was trying to learn about the world of publishing as fast as I could, but I was drowning in sell sheets, ISBN numbers, e-books, backorders and other terminology from the publishing wars. Not to mention bubble wrap. I was up to my ass in bubble wrap. I wished my mentors were here to help. But of course, they were not, and I was all alone, unless you counted my wife who had the official title of Fulfillment Manager for A&M Books—meaning she dragged heavy book cartons to the UPS store. Oh, and a schnauzer worked security.

Anyda Marchant and Muriel Crawford were my mentors and two of the founders of the legendary Naiad Press. They represented more than half a century in the evolution of lesbian literature in America. Their lives spanned almost the entire history of the gay rights movement in this country—thus far, of course. I was lucky enough to know them, love them, learn from them and agree to try, to the best of my ability, to carry on for them.

They were Rehoboth's Gertrude Stein and Alice B. Toklas, serving Dewars scotch instead of marijuana brownies. In the early 1970s, when no novels had happy endings for lesbian stories, Anyda, under the pen name Sarah Aldridge, wrote the novel *The Latecomer* and could not find a publisher. In fact, it was almost dangerous to submit something so outrageous to a mainstream publishing house. *The Latecomer* was the tale of two women finding love together and, scandalously, it had a happy ending.

So, in 1973, Anyda and Muriel, along with two other publishing pioneers, Barbara Grier and Donna McBride, decided to create their own publishing house. They called the publishing house Naiad Press, based on Greek mythology. Naiads were beautiful water nymphs, and Naiad Press would allow lesbian feminist writers' words to flow. Anyda and Muriel put up the $2,000 required to print *The Latecomer*, but no printer would touch a lesbian book with the proverbial ten-foot pole. After several irritating encounters with insulting printers who refused the job, the women finally found a Florida company, whose only other big client was a Baptist Church. "It was a remarkable combination," Anyda said.

The Naiad Press was officially launched on January 1, 1973, with the publication of *The Latecomer* a year later. The printer shipped the finished books to Anyda and Muriel, who distributed them from their garage. "We were shipping clerks," said Muriel.

Anyda, a lawyer with the World Bank, saw to it that by 1974, Naiad was incorporated in Delaware, with Anyda, Muriel, Barbara and Donna as shareholders. Thanks to the large network of independently owned lesbian-feminist bookstores and fledgling gay newspaper outlets cropping up throughout the '70s, Naiad Press started to make a name for itself.

Through the rest of the 1970s and early 80s, Anyda continued to write novels, with Muriel acting as a sounding board and informal editor. In addition to the early Sarah Aldridge novels, Naiad Press began to publish romances, mysteries, and novels by other female authors—writers like Katharine V. Forrest, Renee Vivien, Valerie Taylor and many more.

Anyda was most proud of the business as an incubator for lesbian writers who otherwise might never be published. She and Muriel never expected financial success and never cared if they got any money back on their investments. They used the money made from the sale of *The Latecomer* to pay for the publication of the next book, which in turn financed another. And another.

Over the years, Naiad published eleven Sarah Aldridge novels and dozens of other books by lesbian/feminists—surprisingly growing from a small business in the back of a garage to an impressive feminist publishing company with its own warehouse, staff, author list, and first-rate nationwide reputation.

In the early '80s, Naiad author Jane Rule, who had written the novel *Desert of the Heart*, saw the book turned into the now classic lesbian film *Desert Hearts*. Naiad Press was in the thick of it. In 1985, Naiad also published the ground-breaking and controversial book *Lesbian Nuns: Breaking Silence*, a collection of true stories. But by the late 1980s the Naiad partnership was on the rocks. "Too commercial, not literary," was all Anyda would reveal.

It turned out that Anyda felt Naiad was retreating from its original goal—a publishing opportunity for quality lesbian/feminist writers who might not otherwise be able to publish. Also, as it turned out, the vision Grier and McBride had for the company took Naiad in a much more commercial and controversial direction. In fact, soon after *Lesbian Nuns: Breaking Silence* was released, Naiad Press sold the rights to one of the interviews to *MS Magazine*, which published it in August 1985. Apparently, Naiad, with Grier and McBride at the helm, also sold other stories from the book to the men's magazine *Forum*. The selling of the chapters to *Forum* deeply disturbed Anyda and Muriel on many different levels. Grier's sale of rights to publish excerpts in *Forum* caused a firestorm of controversy within the feminist and lesbian communities, but the controversy also served to make the book a best seller.

Eventually, Barbara Grier and Donna McBride bought Anyda and Muriel out of Naiad Press, and in 1995 Rehoboth's best-known publishers started a new company, A&M Books of

Rehoboth, once again, out of their home and garage. As part of the financial settlement with Naiad, A&M Books retained both the existing stock and the rights to all of the Sarah Aldridge titles.

And Anyda, at 83, was still writing. If nothing else, A&M Books would be the avenue for publishing more Sarah Aldridge novels. Although by this time, the Aldridge novels were joined in gay and mainstream bookstores by an explosion of lesbian-written, lesbian-themed and lesbian-published novels; romances; and the new hot genre, mysteries with lesbian detectives, cops and investigators.

Keeping with the style she knew, Anyda kept on writing. With the lesbian publishing industry growing so rapidly—by this time Naiad was joined by several other successful lesbian publishing outlets—the lesbian community had their own thriving literary culture. And the Sarah Aldridge novels were fast becoming collectible classics.

While continuing to write her romantic novels energized Anyda, her goal was to bring A&M Books to prominence by finding other unpublished authors and letting their words flow as well. The publishers worked together on A&M Books projects every single day for over a decade, at a pace slowed by age, but with more gusto than most people decades younger.

The thirteenth and fourteenth Aldridge novels were released, and they worked to send out publicity, fill orders, and keep the publishing business going. They published the celebrated author Ann Allen Shockley's last book, *Celebrating Hotchclaw*, and published my first book, *As I Lay Frying: a Rehoboth Beach Memoir*. They were both in their 90s and still working.

Anyda's fourteenth Sarah Aldridge novel turned out to be her last. *O, Mistress Mine* was released by A&M Books in 2004 with a big, celebratory book signing party in Rehoboth.

The year 2006 marked the passing of both Anyda and Muriel, within four months of each other—Anyda at age 95 and Muriel at 92. And I inherited A&M Books.

I was flattered, awed, and very much a novice in the publishing world. So, I rolled up my sleeves and became a publisher. My first release was my own *Fried &True: Tales of Rehoboth Beach*. Telling, among other essays, the story of Anyda and Muriel's fifty-seven-year romance with each other. And their great love of publishing and Scotch whisky.

The ladies of Naiad never cared about what it cost—their mission was to publish books written by lesbians and get them into the hands of lesbian readers—who often had nothing else in print that related to their lives. The A&M Books publishing house operated by me had no such luxury. We operated hand to mouth. Or possibly foot in mouth. But either way, investment money we did not have.

But in addition to my two latest essay collections, we managed to publish *The Carousel*, a finely written novel by Stefani Deoul and *Out of Step*, a memoir about a military witch hunt by Lee Watton, with a foreword by Colonel Greta Cammermeyer. We also published the thirty-fifth anniversary edition of *The Latecomer* with commentary by well-known lesbian writers and icons.

Keeping the legacy of Anyda and Muriel, and the Sarah Aldridge novels, alive has been my premier goal with A&M Books. Which is why I was delighted to announce, just recently, that I am teaming up with my esteemed publishing colleagues at Bywater Books. I have become a Bywater author—and Anyda and Muriel's work on the Sarah Aldridge books will live on through Bywater. I couldn't be happier. Or luckier. Or more flattered.

So, this accidental publisher is hanging up her ISBN numbers and bubble wrap to concentrate on writing and performing some of my stories. It's been a grand ride and I await the next chapter. And none of this would have been possible without the ladies of Naiad and their vision that there could and would be happy endings for lesbian literature. Cheers to Anyda and Muriel! Hello to Bywater Books!

JUNE 2017

Celebrating Family

Nothing makes you appreciate the life you have as a friend gone too soon. Our pal Bob Hoffer left the building, but not our hearts or our Facebook pages.

For me, the June 21 celebration of his life was far more than an emotional sendoff for a wonderful person. It was nothing less than an unforgettable affirmation of marriage equality and Rehoboth's enormous community of chosen family.

So no, this column will not be sad. Rather, it's a giddy shout-out to all of us who made the deliberate choice to surround ourselves with our LGBT sisters and brothers (and allies!) to build a world that "gets" us, nurtures creativity, provides as much safety from bigots as possible, and brings us together as a huge, noisy, fun-loving, occasionally squabbling, often frenzied, and always supportive family.

From bears to baby-dykes, lezzies to boy-toys, whether you're butch, femme, young, not so, trans or cis, have certifiables from Ancestry.com or a mutt heritage, whatever your color, religion, or beverage of choice, we are fam-i-ly.

Many of us arrived in town, knowing RB's gay friendly reputation, but knowing no one or, at best, only a handful of people here. Bonnie and I showed up, never having heard of CAMP Rehoboth, never having read *Letters*, wondering if we'd fit in. To borrow a phrase from a friend, as we spent every weekend here for the first few years, "we resided in Maryland, but had a life in Rehoboth."

"You're quitting your job and moving to Delaware? You're insane!" my incredulous father shouted five years later when we broke the news. I struggled to explain the specialness of our lives here, but words failed. A video from last week's service for Bob would have done the trick.

What a community we are. Where else could two retired lesbian teachers wander into CAMP to volunteer to stuff condoms for giveaways at the bars?

Or another now-local couple, on their way to the Carolinas to check out retirement options, stopping by Rehoboth for a single afternoon, meeting an enthusiastic booster in the CAMP courtyard, and immediately changing their plans?

Where else could newly arrived LGBT realtors, newcomer dentists, or first-time authors be fast-tracked to success by such support from a community?

After all, it's an American success story, where two guys from Altoona, PA, can come to town, join a chorus, a church, and a local nonprofit—and less than a decade later have made an indelible mark on the community.

In this special place, when locals are hospitalized, they often receive such hordes of visitors, hospital officials suspect they are harboring celebrities; if tragedy strikes, even strangers pitch in as we become one giant support system.

What's not to love about Drag Volleyball, Broadwalk on the Boardwalk, Sundance, the exploding restaurant scene (and concurrent exploding waistlines), the best independent bookstore in Delaware, classes, art shows, live music every night of the week, Film Festival, Art League? I'm exhausted listing it all much less living it.

Oh, yeah, the beach! And Rehoboth Bay! Happy hours for drinking, or increasingly, in my case, for dinner—just don't call it Early Bird. What the coast offers us is mind-blowing and expanding. All you need to do is reach for it and join in.

As I scanned the church last Wednesday, looking at the crowd and the facilities, I thought, yes, for many of us in the Medicare Club, we're apt to be back here too soon, celebrating the lives of lost family members.

But don't be glum. If it seems there's a lot of illness and loss going around, just remember this one very special thing about living in a small town like Rehoboth: when bad things happen to people, we likely know them, same for good things. That's the nature of our family town.

So even in a troubled world, with threats to our rights, our wallets, our planet, and possibly our lives we must remember to look around and celebrate the wondrous events, opportunities, people, love, and freedom we have here.

Let's take every opportunity to enjoy each other's company, take part in the fun stuff, get involved, and live it the heck up. As my father also said (when he got over the shock of the Delaware thing), "You only live once, and if you do it right, once is enough."

Let's continue to do it right, my friends. In my book *Fried and Convicted*, my bio ends with "Fay and Bonnie are aging in place on a boardwalk bench in Rehoboth Beach." Meet us there for some caramel popcorn. WE ARE FAM-I-LY.

JULY 2017

Travel Bingo: Everything Old is New Again

Bingo is not my thing.

I only went to a bingo hall once. I bought three game cards, the least you could buy, and had no idea how I'd handle even that.

I sat between two frail-looking elderly women who appeared to know their way around a bingo game. They were gum-popping, chain-smoking bingo biddies who each had forty-eight game cards in front of them. Forty-eight!

When the first game began, they dabbed their total of ninety-six cards with the permanent marker digit dabber, then swooped in to mark mine before I realized my card contained the number called. I got wind burn from their sleeves and couldn't dodge the dabbers dappling my forearms like a Jackson Pollock canvas.

Permanently marked in bright splotches, I watched the frantic bingo mania around me, quickly gave up, and never darkened a Bingorama door again.

So, Bingo is not my thing. Neither is a boring road trip. But combine the two and we're in business.

Remember Travel Bingo? At age eleven, in the back seat of our 1959 Buick (yes, I'm *that* old), my sister and I had Travel Bingo cards. It was our parents' way to quell our incessant "Are we there yet?" inquiries. We played between stops at Howard Johnson's.

The cards housed a classic bingo board, but instead of numbers, the squares were filled with drawings of cows, bridges, railroad crossings, and signs depicting No U-Turn, speed limit, and men working. Once you spied one of the sights, there was a little plastic window to slide over the drawing on the square.

Did you play, too?

Well, with air travel such a mess these days, we're driving more. Besides, our schnauzer Windsor gets to come along.

So, I was thrilled to discover that our local Rehoboth toy and gadget emporium stocks retro Travel Bingo cards. Yup, they look and feel just like the originals, down to the orange plastic window sliders. Of course, they are $5, not forty-nine cents and the speed limit graphics proclaim 65 not 45. Sadly, both the old and new cards have the same "men working" graphic. A half a century later I would have hoped for more gender neutralness.

Clutching our newly purchased bingo cards, we headed out, launching both the trip and the game. Those little plastic windows got quite a workout as we spied horses and sports cars and speed limit signs. "Silo!" and "Motor home!" we'd shout. "Airport!" and "Motorcycle!" It was a lot more fun than PBS *Cartalk*. Between us we shouted "Bingo!" for the first time just outside Philly.

In the next round, oddly enough, the one tough "get" along the New Jersey Turnpike was a Coke sign. Most fast-food places and billboards show a generic cola. We finally passed a Coke logo on a Chik-fil-A sign, but I hesitated to use it as we are boycotting the chain. Heck, I slid the plastic window over anyway. What principles?

The game dragged on as we came over the George Washington Bridge and up I-95. Not a silo to be seen. Nor a horse, for that matter. Although Windsor snorted and barked like a Doberman when we passed a horse trailer. So, we agreed that a horse trailer, even without the sight of an actual horse's ass, was acceptable.

Oh, I could go so many places with the horse's ass comment, but somehow it led us to postulate about an adult version of Travel Bingo. We could fill the card with drawings of Vape stores and billboards for vasectomies, fireworks, and ambulance-chasing lawyers. How about sightings of roadkill, prisons, and adult bookstores? We could be X-rated Travel Bingo entrepreneurs, closing the little windows while shouting "Lap dances!" I vowed to investigate a patent.

Seriously, we love the game. Our journeys have flown by even as we travel by ground transportation. The trips seem shorter and more fun thanks to Travel Bingo.

In fact, while it helps pass the time on the road, it can also add a bit of fun to everyday wanderings. Somehow the game stays stuck in our psyche when we're home and out doing errands, shopping, or even going for ice cream along Route 9. We point and yell "Silo!" We cannot help ourselves. "Bridge!" in Bethany, "Railroad!" in Lewes, "Parking Meter!" in Rehoboth. Okay, that last one is not on the card.

It's okay if passersby think we're nuts. You don't stop playing because you get old; you get old because you stop playing.

AUGUST 2017

Ready, Set, Gurgitate!

I may have missed my calling.

On a Monday morning following a carb-loading boardwalk binge, I happened on an article about competitive eating. I learned it's an actual sport, with its own professional association called Major League Eating. Who knew?

Sure, I'd heard about the legendary Nathan's Hot Dog Eating Contest, but figured it was a gluttonous anomaly. Wrong.

By definition, "Competitive eating, or speed eating, is defined as an activity in which participants compete to consume large quantities of food in a short time period." Puleeze. After two decades in Rehoboth, I'm a champ, specializing in the pizza, fries, frozen custard trifecta.

As for beat the clock, ever try getting your supper served quickly in a tourist-packed restaurant and still make a movie? Speed eating, for sure.

But these professional contests are typically only eight to ten minutes long, with the person consuming the most food declared the winner and taking home the big, big prize money.

When we amateurs rush to consume our boardwalk fries before the attack of the dive-bombing seagulls, our only prize is world-class reflux.

It was the range of foods in these contests that stunned me. Aside from Nathan's, you can compete with Chicken Wings ("Winner downs 250 Hooters wings in 10 minutes!"), Vienna sausages, Moon Pies, Ebelskivers (Danish Pancakes like donut holes), or get ready, Slugburgers in Corinth, Mississippi. Fortunately, these do not contain actual crawly slugs, but are hamburgers fattened up by bread and other meat extenders.

Major League sanctioned events run the gamut from World

Taco champs, Sweet Corn Chomping, Corned Beef on Rye contests, Oyster-gulping and international ice cream trials. Then there's the World Gyoza Eating Championships. Gyozas are Japanese wanton wrappers containing pork and cabbage. I wouldn't want to be at *that* Vanity Fair after-party.

Some of the contests add challenges to interfere with speed, like eating with two spoons or with no hands. That happened to me last week when I dropped my fork in Southwest's economy class.

And there are special techniques utilized in competitive eating, like "Chipmunking," when professional eaters attempt to stuff as much food in their mouths as possible during the final seconds of a contest. If this skill is permitted, eaters are then given two minutes to swallow the food or risk demerits.

I'd risk requiring the Heimlich Maneuver. And can you see me, cheeks puffed like trumpeter Louie Armstrong, with so much food stashed it would take two minutes to clear out? I don't have room in there for a dentist's cotton ball, much less a mouthful of Slugburgers. I don't know how Alvin and the Chipmunks do it.

And "Dunking" is when the pros are permitted to dunk foods in water or other liquids to soften them to make them easier to swallow. Hell, if you dunk ice in vodka, it makes everything in life easier to swallow.

If, in the course of human events, a competitor regurgitates (I'm sorry. You weren't reading this at lunch, were you?), ESPN and the Nathan's Hot Dog folks deem that the Reversal of Fortune Rule. It's the corollary to what goes up must come down and is an automatic disqualification.

And, like all athletes, rigorous personal training takes place to stretch stomach capacity. Without knowing it, I've been training since kindergarten. Get this, competitors commonly train by drinking large amounts of water over a short time. The heck with that. Give me large amounts of tiramisu.

So, too, in this world of intestinal fortitude (the phrase used literally for once), there are superstars and groupies. Big crowds have been showing up at these binge fests since 1916 at the first Nathan's Hot Dog Contest—brainchild of a new sales manager. Oh, what marketing hath wrought. Last year, 40,000 people showed up to Coney Island to watch the conspicuous consumption.

Not only do folks watch and cheer, but the champs are superstars. Joey Chestnut is recognized by Major League Eating as ranked first in the world. On July 4, 2017, he took first prize (lots of money and, I hope, a case of Pepcid) when he was crowned hot dog champ by knocking back 72 frankfurters. Way to cut the mustard, Joey!

Now, fans and competitors travel internationally on the Competitive Eating circuit. It's like the Tour de Lunch, or the Alka Seltzer Open (seriously, ESPN broadcasts that one) have exploded in popularity. I'm expecting an invitation to the International Bust a Gut Games.

No thanks, I'll just stay in Delaware, retaining rank amateur status, enjoying the occasional boardwalk binge, crab feast or better yet, a sensible meal at some of the culinary coast's finest restaurants.

The mere thought of my recent gustatory gluttony makes me want to, well, commit a reversal of fortune. So, I'm having a small salad for lunch.

But I have no doubt I'll be back in competition mode by the weekend. Funnel Cake anyone?

AUGUST 2017

Applying Myself

I am officially too old to apply for a job.

They wanted a resume. Hah! Last time I put one together was 1999. As for work history, I got finger spasms from typing and only went back twenty-two years (which was the day Steve Elkins hired me to write for this publication).

And which of my jobs should I highlight? I've been an Executive Director, the Easter Bunny, and chief chocolate taster. I've hawked tourism, books, bars, and bagels. I've been a newspaper editor, theatrical director, author, and publisher. I broke into show biz at an age when I would more likely break a hip. You get to be old, you've done stuff.

Then the application called for my college transcripts, and I howled. Will FedEx ship the stone tablets they were chiseled on? Hasn't the parchment already disintegrated? I'll let you know how I fare talking to the registrar's office. I haven't used the word registrar in almost half a century.

Oy. I was having psychedelic undergrad flashbacks. At least my long-term memory is still working.

Next came all the application pages I had to sign and initial, including the drug-free schools, and workplace policy. I had to read all the punishments for being found with controlled substances or drug paraphernalia. Wow, I hope that doesn't include the bong I now use as a planter.

And boy, it's a good thing I didn't have to initial this thing in 1967. Currently, I'm unstoked by controlled substances, but I'm still marching in the streets for pretty much the same issues. How is this fair?

And I am so out of the loop. The appendix of controlled substances included drugs I'd never even heard of. But thanks to the workplace policy, I now know how long I'd be in the cast of *Orange Is the New Black* if caught with any of them.

Moving right along in my application process, I loved having to initial the Pregnant Workers Fairness Act. It told me they would make reasonable accommodations if I got pregnant or was lactating. Okay, try to get the picture of me holding a suckling baby out of your mind.

But if I were pregnant or nursing, they wouldn't have to make accommodations for me anyway, as I would make a fortune by selling my story to the tabloids. "Sixty-Eight-Year-Old Gives Birth!" The real story would be that it wasn't a schnauzer.

Okay, so I initialed all the spots required and then considered putting a big N/A on the page and circling it. I actually wrote N/A/U, for No Actual Uterus.

But seriously, I love that Delaware law protects pregnant and nursing women. That sure didn't happen in the '60s. We've come a long way baby (or with babies), but, as we all know, we've still got a long way to go. Misogyny thrives.

More and more places are trying to fight it. And they are doing a great job battling sexual harassment in schools and the workplace (except for Fox News). In fact, part of my application for work also included completing online courses in Sexual Harassment and Eliminating Violence in the Workplace. Luckily, these were not based on the syllabus by Dr. Bill Cosby.

The online courses were thoughtful and well-designed discussions of the dos and don'ts of personal interaction. After reading the material and answering the questions, nobody should be clueless about what constitutes bad behavior.

We certainly did not have discussions like this when I was in college or in my first job. It might have prevented my having to slap my blind date silly in that Karmann Ghia sportster parked along the roadway in Rock Creek Park one dark night in the bad old days. Or later, having to leave a job at a DC television station because the atmosphere was toxic with sexual innuendo, and supervisors wanting a lot more from employees than work product.

So we really have come a long way on a lot of topics since I got my very first job at that TV station, where I typed fifty-five words a minute on an IBM Selectric, writing press releases and promos for the princely sum of $110.00 a week. The telephone operator still had one of those plug-in systems like Lily Tomlin's Ernestine used ("Is this the party to whom I'm speaking???") and my job application consisted of a two-page document and a five-minute interview. I was asked my age. If I had a car. If I planned on getting pregnant. And if I'd mind making the coffee each morning.

Oh, how times, and I, have changed. And the good thing about this upcoming very part-time temporary job is that it involves no alarm clocks, no dress-for-success clothing, a five-minute commute, and doing what I love.

Now when will those fossil transcripts arrive? Will they be suitable for carbon-dating? Will the Smithsonian want them?

I graduated two score and seven years ago. I cannot wait to see my grade-point average and the list of classes I little noted nor long remembered. But I will always remember what I did there. And it was groovy.

AUGUST 2017

Aging Gracelessly, All Ears

Or so it seems.

For readers over fifty, remember when the invitations to join AARP started arriving in the mail? It was a real come to dentures moment. My forty-eight-year-old mate was doubly aggravated because the invitation was for both of us.

Time marched on, through fifteen years of unsolicited ads for auxiliary life insurance, full-body diagnostic scans, and retirement planning. Then came retirement itself, with the tsunami of envelopes advertising supplemental Medicare insurance.

As retirees, within the last four years, we've gotten a deluge of coupons for adult diapers sure to stem any deluge, warnings about scams targeting the elderly, and propaganda about lounge chairs that eject you to a standing position. Lately, though, the mail has been trending toward invitations for complimentary hearing aid tests.

Say again?

Hell, I used to be on lists for complimentary concert tickets and backstage passes. Now it's free audiology parties. I won't hear of it!

Which may be the point.

I came home one day last week, stood on the porch fumbling for my house key and realized I could hear the blaring *Jeopardy* theme through the front window. After the first question, I was pretty sure my neighbors would answer "What is: 'old farts next door?'"

Once inside, I realized how loud we'd had the sound up for the dog. I expected to see him greet us with earplugs. Okay, maybe we were boosting the sound on the TV a little higher than in the past. Maybe we should do the mature thing and check out the audiology invitation. Nah . . .

We got TV Ears. Bluetooth devices for blue hairs. We almost didn't get them, as their internet spokesgeezer is the eternally wholesome and proselytizing Pat Boone. I wondered if, when you turn on the headphones, you hear strains of "April Love."

But I got past Pat and his joyous contention that "TV Ears Saved My Marriage!" Presumably the $59 set comes with a pair of sound-clarifying earphones for the couple where one spouse jacks up the volume to excruciating levels and the other spouse files for divorce. Not our problem. We are both equally guilty of asking "can you turn that up?" to whichever of us has custody of the remote.

So, we ordered the dual set of TV Ears ($79). They come in a handy little charging and transmitting station. Plug it into the wall socket, and the audio-out jack on the TV and you're all set. According to Mr. Goody-Two-White-Buck-Shoes, you sit back and there's "peace and harmony in the house."

Not so fast. Although we could each hear the TV soundtrack quite clearly, adjusting our own volume, that jabbering 1950s heartthrob neglected to tell us that the rest of the world would be entirely dead to us.

Me: "Wow, wasn't Kiefer Sutherland great in that scene?"
Mate: "What?"
Me: "Can you hear better with these?"
Mate: "What?"
Mate: "Do we have any popcorn?"
Me: "What?"

No peace, no harmony, no popcorn. And we missed the dog barking to go out. What if something else needed our attention?

Mate: "It's the Zombie Apocalypse! A nine-foot Yeti is about to whack you with a hatchet."
Me: "What?"

It was like being in the proverbial cone of silence. TV Ears are great if you watch alone. But then, who needs them? Just batten the windows and crank up the volume.

The use of TV Ears forces the question "Do I want to hear the TV but not my spouse or schnauzer?" What's more important, deciphering the *Jeopardy* question or putting my marriage into that state? Understanding the dialogue on *Scandal* or causing one? Plainly hearing *Animal Planet* or turning my living room into one?

It's an eardrum conundrum of deafening proportions.

So, we tried TV viewing with only one earbud of the two on the headset plugged into our heads. You don't wear them like traditional over-the-head sets. These plug into your ears and sit under your chin. While we looked totally ridiculous wearing half a dangling headset, we could listen for ambient commentary with the free ear.

Then we had to change seats, so our unplugged ambient ears faced each other. The whole dangling headset, musical chairs action set us to laughing so hard we took off the silly headsets and cranked up the TV. We wondered whether the neighbors would prefer *Madame Secretary* or *Call the Midwife*. Just so long as they wouldn't call the police.

Okay, okay, I'm off to walk the dog and go to the mailbox to see if there's an invitation for a free audiology visit. Be right back.

(Ten minutes later)

I don't know whether to laugh or cry. Today's gift from the postal service includes (and this would be bad enough) the Senior Comforts catalog featuring compression socks, tripod cane tips, and bunion shields. Okay, I might be interested in the Twistee Jar Opener.

But here's the corker. We got an attractive invitation-like envelope and inside was an advertisement for the security and peace of mind offered by freaking Pre-Paid Cremation!!! UNCLE!!!!!!

I was so incredulous I tore out of the house, jumped on my bike (okay, my adult Trike), and peddled off into the sunset.

Mate: "When schmuf, muffled, bwabwa, muffled, you, muffled, muffled."

Me: (calling over my shoulder) What?????

Well yesterday, the ads in the mailbox took an even darker turn.

Stop it!!!!!!!

AUGUST 2017

Not Down in the Dumps

Just last week there was an article in the *New York Times* about parents downsizing and how none of their children want any of the "stuff." It was an abstract concept to me until this week.

Bonnie and I are at my stepmother's home in New York, a house she shared with my father for more than thirty years. Sitting in the den, I realized that in his own meticulous, sophisticated way, my father had been a champion packrat.

No, their beautifully decorated home, filled with mid-century modern designer furniture and glorious artwork was not your typically cluttered and filthy A&E *Hoarders* house. And yet...

The bookshelves held a massive collection of art books, typography manuals, World War II histories, baseball encyclopedias, coffee-table tomes, and other dusty, unopened-for-decades volumes that would have to go somewhere someday.

With my stepmom contemplating downsizing, someday meant now, when we were around to assist.

The local library offered good news: they'd take used books for resale.

Massive, stunning art books, with full-color prints by Chagall, Miro, and Lautrec, made their way to the back of our SUV. I dropped a Compendium of Contemporary Art on my foot, only to discover that, in this case, "contemporary" meant seventy-five years ago. Truly contemporary was the swelling bruise on my pinky toe.

We unloaded six hefty hardback dictionaries, two thesauruses (Thesauri?), four "encyclopedias of" things like English lit, baseball stats, public speaking quips, and Movie Trivia, all rendered completely archaic by Google. In fact, I just got the word *archaic* instead of *obsolete* compliments of my computer screen.

Among the books considered for disposal were several paperbacks with titles like *Conquering the Paper Pile-Up*, *Not for Packrats Only*, *Don't be a Hoarder!*, and other clutterati. That my stepmom decided to keep those showed her complicity in the problem.

As for that paper pile-up, we tackled boxes in the garage and excavated six cartons plus three file drawers of my father's work product.

As former Creative Director for the CBS network, he was on the 1950s team that designed the CBS eye logo. So we found dozens of logo "mechanicals" looking at us. In case you are not ancient like me, a mechanical is a hard copy drawing of the famous eye with words (ordered from a type house) glued on, plus overlays of colored gels taped over it all. Photoshop or In-Design now makes mechanicals superfluous (also a googled word). There were hundreds of copies of the celebrity retina in various colors, sizes, configurations. None bloodshot, like mine, from the delving and dust.

A few years ago, I contacted CBS and the Museum of Broadcasting and asked if they wanted any of the "stuff." They said they had plenty. Likewise, there was not a market on eBay, so . . . out to the back of the car went the hundreds of CBS eyeballs, full-page *New York Times* ads for *Gunsmoke*, *Hogan's Heroes*, *The Beverly Hillbillies*, and *The Ed Sullivan Show* with the Beatles and the Rolling Stones. There were booklets advertising the CBS fall line-ups to advertisers, syndication ads for *Mary Tyler Moore* ("Moore for Less!") and hundreds of *TV Guide* ads for *The Carol Burnett Show*, *The Lucy Show*, and the rest of my childhood.

Now you have to know I spent hours going through this "stuff" in case I could find an ad from 1957's live CBS production of *Cinderella* with Julie Andrews. I do believe she was my first lesbian crush. I was nine. But no luck. That ad I would have kept, framed, and worshipped.

We filled the back of the car twice with all the paperwork. I loved looking through my television history and yes, I did keep a few things. Shhh, Bonnie doesn't know. I snagged an old Route 66 ad, because George Maharis was my last heterosexual crush and that show gave me my love for mid-sixties Corvettes.

Out, too, went books upon books of printing color charts (now online), and long lists and examples of 10-, 12-, and 14-point typefaces, like Bodoni and Avant Garde. My father not only used those "new" typefaces, but went to three-martini lunches with the man who designed them. Much of this work was from the Mad Men era, fascinating to see, but overwhelming to keep.

In addition, we added to the dump load thousands of carefully saved photo negatives and duplicate or not-so-great photos from my childhood. How happy was I to toss the photo of a grimacing seven-year-old me in a tutu?

My parents ordered me to take ballet lessons, thinking it might make me, like my sister, more interested in cosmetics than cowgirls. The plot, of course, failed. So not only have I spared you that tutu photo, but also the one of me grinning in the Roy Rogers cowboy hat and holstered six guns.

I had already inherited all the photo albums with similar photos, so out went these duplicate baby pictures, school photos, and photographic evidence that I was already a baby dyke in 1956.

So too, did we have to pitch a huge carton of my father's old family photos. I would have loved to save these old-fashioned formal portraits of my elders, but not a single one had a name on the back. Since there's no one living to identify them, sadly, out they went.

If there's one lesson to pass along, please ID all your photos on the back. Nobody else ever needs to go through a box of photos, looking at the faces of hundreds of unknown ancestors.

So, it was quite a purge.

In the end, we paid $40 to deposit 300 to 500 pounds of trash at the dump. We dropped off three more trunk loads, much heavier than the dump-load, to the used book bins at the library. My guess is we unloaded about a ton of "stuff." Maybe more.

The house is less cluttered, and I sit here with an ice bag on my left shoulder rotator cuff. My pinky toe remains bright purple.

But the world has been deprived of one more photo of me in a tutu. Rejoice!

AUGUST 2017

Out the Windows, into Cyberspace

Hello, I am speaking to you from password hell.

Was it my birthday, my schnauzer's birthday, special character (human), special character (keyboard), a Yiddish word—what the heck did I use for that password?

I got a new computer. And among other indignities, I had to log in with my password the first time I opened every single application on the machine. Yes, I have a list, but in my dotage, I may have forgotten to log in a few password resets, so my whole day was spent resetting passwords and saying naughty words, some of which became passwords.

It was bad enough when I needed a password with a capital letter and numbers. Now we need to add semicolons and ampersands, percent signs and the ubiquitous @.

Random choices are the only solution, because once you start trying to make passwords make sense to provide you with a clue, you are on your way to the loony bin.

Banking: Overdrawn100$ (see, a cap letter, a number, *and* a special character!)

Amazon: Killingretail75%

Facebook: Rabbithole24/7

AARP: 69&Aginginplace@Rehoboth

But what good are passwords when any robber entering my office can find them all in 14-point type, thumbtacked to the wall? Or in a tidy list on my phone? Frankly, I figure we need only one killer password for the phone and a deadbolt on the front door.

Okay, I get it. If our election can be hacked by Russians, my Facebook account can be hacked by a labradoodle. But why? So, they can take pictures of their lunch and say it was me? If I could figure out how to monetize my Facebook account, I would. If they do so under my name, will I get royalties? More LIKES? Paparazzi?

As if password purgatory wasn't bad enough, I had to learn Windows10 on my new PC. I've been avoiding this for years, nursing my elderly Windows 7 computer through various maladies and viruses. It finally died and Amazon had to be notified.

Within thirty-six hours I had a spanking new machine and no idea how to earn a living. I can see the Windows 10 advertising slogans now:

> *Why use one key stroke when you can use two!*
> *We've hidden your most-used icons!*
> *Just Do It—if you can figure out how!*

I could not. Windows 10 made me want to jump from one. And no schpritz with Windex could clean up my mess. So, I called HP tech help. A thoroughly nice fellow ("I'm Mike") with an Indian accent asked permission to work on my machine to set up my printer. Suddenly, the cursor took off as if possessed as Magic Mike clicked, checked, cut, pasted and organized my PC as if he was Rosemary's Baby on a rampage.

I got the yips thinking about Mike's happy hands trolling inside my computer from half a world away. Creepy. And we thought Marconi and the transatlantic cable were a big deal.

Think of the possibilities. Mike could sign me up for *Breitbart News*, access my bank account (he'd be disappointed) or, if he really wanted to be helpful, write this column for me.

But no, he merely hooked up my printer to my wireless router. When I seized control (without incident or exorcism), Mike asked me to fill out some registration information and follow his commands to finish the setup.

I did as I was instructed, and was met with this: "Wowee,

you have very excellent keyboard skills Miss Fay and follow commands very quickly for a person of your age."

I didn't know if I should pat myself on the back or cyberslap him.

Bidding a fond farewell to India, I downloaded several more programs, meeting my Waterloo at Quicken, which would not download no matter how hard I tried. Back on the phone I let the Quicken computer whisperer put his grubby little fingers inside my computer as well. Naturally, all this "help" cost money and my on-sale computer quickly became the biggest loser.

I've now managed to fumble through this document, in twice the time it normally takes, double-clicking where one used to do, cursing while trying to find the *italics* icon, and being completely baffled by the unrecognizable graphics, quite tiny, I might add on my tool bar.

Hmmm ... bar. It's very nearly five o'clock, Hell, happy hour's been and gone half a world away. I think I'll have a cocktail before trying to decipher my new email configuration to send this column out to my editor.

Happily, my bar has no password. But if it did, it would be: Windows10droveme2drink#!&%$

MAY 2017

Infotainment! And This Time It's a Good Thing

It's a really good thing there was no television and screenwriter's strike.

Sure, I love the shows I watch regularly and would miss my dose of escapist stories and late-night comedy if there was a writer's walk-out. But there's a whole lot more important reason I'm glad they did not strike.

Those writers are a huge part of our national political resistance movement. These days my shows are less escapist and more in your face. A slew of progressive writers are having a grand time advocating for the resistance—or at least the hot-button issues progressives see as under attack.

These crafty and very talented writers are sneaking their personal values and pet issues into episodic television at a dizzying rate. I suppose our red and blue societal split has now completely infiltrated our TV habits as thoroughly as it has opened fault lines in our maps, communities, and friendships—or former friendships.

So, television writers have taken up their causes. We're all used to cop shows coming up with scripts that are "ripped from the headlines!" but these latest examples are more "ripped from the editorial pages!"

Last week, *Law & Order: SVU* had an uncannily familiar story about fake news sending a lone gunman to free underage sex-slaves from the basement of a pizza place. Familiar, right? In this case, dear Mariska Hargitay was, for once, not being threatened by bad guys, almost raped by badder guys, cussed out by her superiors, or being saved from death by Ice-T (the person, not the drink). This time she was railing against fake news and how dangerous that is. I loved it.

Likewise, on *Designated Survivor*, while the Capitol building sat in rubble and assassins aligned to pick off favorite characters, the show took a detour for a subplot about arts funding. Seriously, it's odd and refreshing at the same time.

Do you watch *Madame Secretary*? In between concocted tales of scary international incidents and hostage situations come pointed comments about the reality of climate change and need for freedom of the press.

Sure, large social issues have been in series' plots since *All in the Family, Maude, Golden Girls, Cagney and Lacey*, and so many more. Of course, entire series like the marvelous *Dear White People* (Netflix), *Modern Family*, and the returning *Will and Grace* tackle race, religion, and LGBT issues all the time.

But this new rush to add my kind of family values to scripted TV seems more urgent, more immediate, more comforting than ever. It's like those writers (and producers and casts) are putting on their pink pussy hats and standing on a soapbox even as they entertain us.

I say good.

We cannot have too much resistance. And television's participation in this cultural moment when nobody can stop talking about the assault on our democracy fits right in. After all, none of us can shut up these days about the family of rich elephants in the room. Not for an entire hour at the dining table, not at intermission in the theatre, not at a restaurant, the gym, or the carpool. Not even during a killer card game. The conversation always comes back to those elephants.

In fact, I know of no other time, six-months after a presidential election, when so much of our social discourse has been spent in fearful, angry, incredulous conversation about disturbing current events. I'm pretty sure it's not just me. I mean everybody I talk to is suffering from post-election depression, ranging from mild and manageable to massive and debilitating.

I'm heading for the dentist with two cracked teeth because

for the first time in my long life I am grinding my teeth in my sleep. I know whose fault that is. I am in favor of hiring a special prosecutor to investigate the family whose name I'd rather not mention just so I can keep my teeth from falling out.

Even I was shocked the other day when I told someone that gay rights had slipped from first on my activist agenda down to seventh or eighth behind saving our democracy, fighting for Mother Earth, protecting public schools, and staving off the day when dystopian novels become current events.

All this having been said, you see why I'm happy there was no writer's strike. I need those shout-outs about climate change, journalistic honesty, and arts funding. I need to hear hope and cohesiveness from my smart TV. It will help keep up the momentum for taking back our democracy.

Next up, will we hear about the deportation of tax-paying immigrants on *Madame Secretary*, or overzealous actions by Homeland Security on *NCIS: New Orleans*?

Right now, you can't escape politics in escapist TV. And I don't want to.

JANUARY 2018

Cyclone Snow Bomb 1, Yeti 0

It was a snow-i-cane. I'm not telling anybody who was in Delaware January 3-7 anything new here. I bet everybody has a story about being snowbound; being bone-chilling cold; and worrying about their pipes, literal and figurative, freezing.

In my case, I had to face the snow bomb cyclone alone, as Bonnie drove to Philly on the eve of the impending blizzard and got stranded there. I, on the other hand, awoke that Thursday morning to a four-foot snow drift blocking my front door. And it was seventeen degrees out.

Heading to the rear of the house I managed to pry open the inward-swinging back door to stare at the north face of Kilimanjaro. And back to the pleading face of the dog. Alas, Windsor stood there, trying to be a good boy.

Dear readers, this was a job for which I was ill-prepared. For going on thirty-six years now, I have had a resident shoveler. Certainly, I used to help, but let's face it, my contribution tended toward providing Swiss Miss.

I donned two pair of Alaskan souvenir socks; two pairs of sweatpants (which, for their first time might experience actual sweat); a long-sleeved shirt, topped with a hoodie cinched around my head; and my puffy Eddie Bauer coat. I didn't know whether I looked like a *South Park* cartoon or the Abominable Snowman. I went to put on shoes but could not bend over. What followed was Old Frankenstein walking stiff-legged, then force-folding myself into a chair to try to reach my feet to tie my laces. I may have heard Windsor chuckling.

Finally ready, mittened hands grabbing the show shovel, I carved my way down the back steps, flinging snow and battling my way into the yard. I could have used crampons and climbing rope. By the time I hacked through Everest and cleared a square foot doggie comfort station I was panting so hard I was a human snow blower. If only.

So, I looked back at Windsor and called for him to come down the steps. He U-turned and ran for the sofa.

I waddled back up the steps and lumbered into the house as if Windsor had invited the neighborhood Yeti for lunch. I grabbed the dog, held him under my arm like an inflated Carson Wentz, and went back outside. The second his schnauzer paws touched the ground he turned tail and raced back into the house.

Dammit. I wobbled after him, grabbed his leash, and burst into hysterics from the act of trying to attach a leash to a collar while wearing baseball-glove-sized mittens. But this time I had him. We both went back to base camp; he could not escape, and business was conducted.

As I looked around the postage stamp yard, I realized that both gates opened outward and were also thoroughly blocked by ginormous drifts. I was, indeed, completely snowbound.

Now I have never been claustrophobic. By this time Bonnie would have dug her way out with a spoon if she had to. But not me. However, there's something about the sheer silence of a snowbound neighborhood with nobody moving—no cars, no plows, no bird sounds, no nothing, which gave me the yips. In case of emergency, I was seriously trapped.

I tried to put it out of my mind, avoiding the Weather Channel and CNN, both of which made me think of various states of emergency. I binged on *Law and Order: SVU*, I read a lesbian romance novel, and I played iPad Bubble Buster. But I couldn't shake my discomfort.

So, I put a stepstool against the front window, checked how wide I could open it (dubiously wide enough for Bigfoot) and figured how to punch out the screen. Picturing myself climbing up, thrusting a leg out the window, trying to haul the rest of me out, so I could flop into a snow angel on the porch gave me odd comfort.

I spent the next two days eating leftover matzo ball soup, watching TV shows I like but Bonnie doesn't, and wishing Windsor was a slightly better conversationalist.

I fielded dozens of calls from pals asking if I was all right and made many such calls in return. I learned that my neighborhood is chock full of generous, energetic people, several with snow blowers, and I was tickled to have a crew show up by late Friday to dig me out.

My spouse returned Friday evening, and we hibernated all day Saturday, feeling our joints calcifying from lack of activity. By Saturday night I was chasing Windsor around the dining room table yelling "Gimme that toy!" just to get myself moving. We didn't brave driving until Sunday morning, and even then, conditions remained crappy, with frigid temps.

But I survived the snow-i-cane. Next year it's Florida right after the holidays. We stayed too long at the fair.

JANUARY 2018

Good Moose Hunting

I laughed out loud when I got the email about the moose sighting. And face it, laughter these days is medicinal.

My snortfest came when a friend forwarded an article about moose (that's plural) taking up residence in Nevada. And since I have a writer's event there shortly, she thought I might finally get to see a moose in the wild.

Fat chance. Fat, antlered chance.

Though I long to see one of these spectacular creatures in person (or would that be in-moose?) and have had several chances to do so, I've been shut out from a face to muzzle moose meeting.

And I'm starting to feel a real kinship with these beasts. At my age, with my neck waddle, I resemble a moose with that flap of skin known as a bell swaying beneath its moose throat. I want to commiserate.

And did you know that moose are grazers and will casually devour seventy-three pounds of vegetation a day in the summer and thirty-four pounds in the winter? I can do that on Harry and David's Popcorn Moose Munch.

Years ago, in Alaska, the state with more moose than any other, we came up empty hoofed. All I wanted to do was whistle and shout "What a rack!" But no. We saw moose sculptures, stuffed moose heads, and antlered winter hats but zilch live moose. Although I did purchase a souvenir moose bobblehead for my dashboard.

In the Canadian Rockies, near Banff, moose sightings are legendary. Not for me. I thought I saw one out the window of the Fairmont Hotel Bar, but it turned out to be a hallucination compliments of a chocolate mousse martini. I did, however come home with a moose plush toy dressed like a Canadian Mountie.

When touring Nova Scotia's Cabot Trail, every roadside shop sold moose memorabilia. Any moose sightings? Nope. How can that be when there are more seven-foot, 1,000-pound moose there than people? But I did stop by a gift shop to buy a moose antler backscratcher.

I even spent dusk, then dark, on multiple days, staring from the car window into wet boggy areas. After a couple of hours, all I saw was double.

One time in Maine, at a scenic overlook, we peered through a telescope onto the mountain of trees and pond-filled glades below. Squinting, I saw a bunch of small brown objects below, but between my eyesight and the distance, they could have been that stuff bears do in the woods.

I came home from the trip with a faux Moose Crossing sign for my yard, but no real moose having crossed any of my paths.

These beasts also roam freely in the White Mountains of New Hampshire, where we drove through mountain roads, and passed multiple bright yellow Moose-in-Road warning signs. Nada.

Then we spent a ridiculous amount of money on a minibus Moose Safari Tour, where the company boasted of seeing moose on nearly 1,000 of their tours in their ten-year history.

We gawked out the picture windows for two interminable hours, seeking beady-little moose eyes in the woods. At one point, at a bathroom stop our tour guide said, "I have a feeling we're going to see a moose tonight."

At which point some poor schmuck in a moose suit boarded the bus, waving and blowing kisses. Please dear God, make him vamoose.

From there, I learned about Moose Jaw, Saskatchewan, where my odds of achieving moose meet-up would rise. But I demurred since the resourceful Moose Jaw locals are the undisputed champs of repurposing one of their most abundant natural resources: moose droppings. Products include moose-nugget earrings, moose nugget key rings, tie tacks, Mooseltoe for the holidays, and 14-carat gold-plated moose nuggets.

I knew better than to let myself loose in a Moose Jaw Souvenir shop.

But now, Nevada looms.

The state appears to be home to a small but growing number of gangly moose, or ungulates—a term for hoofed animals, not to be confused with undulates, which is what a Vegas showgirl does. These ungulates (I love writing that word) must have migrated across the badlands and down into Nevada. No longer are there just Canada Snow Geese, but now Canada Snow Meese (an alternative plural).

But does Las Vegas offer me one last chance? I'm not betting on it. Since most of Nevada is desert, with little moose habitat, my chances of seeing a moose snorting in the wild there are about as great as my winning a million-dollar jackpot at the Golden Nugget.

Hey, wait a minute. What's inside those golden nuggets?

I'm switching my accommodations to Ballys and giving up moose hunting for tickets to Cirque du Soleil. Much better odds. And no undulating ungulates with gold-plated droppings. Although, in Vegas, you never know.

MARCH 2018

For Steve Elkins

Authors Note: this is the eulogy I gave at the memorial service for CAMP Rehoboth Executive Director Steve Elkins, who passed away after a hard-fought battle with lymphoma.

Good morning. It's very likely that with the exception of Steve's biological family and pre-Delaware friends, many of the more than 400 people here today would not even be living in, visiting, or enjoying the diverse, welcoming community of Rehoboth Beach if it were not for Steve Elkins and his devoted husband, Murray Archibald. And those who are natives or who came here before the 1990s, have seen their lives enhanced and forever changed by this man as well.

And while dear Murray, over this past quarter century, shared and continues to share his creative genius with us, it was Steve Elkins, through years of quiet diplomacy, reaching out, bravely jumping into messy situations, who made this portion of Sussex County the safe haven it is today. I like to call it Gayberry, RFD.

Steve was my dear friend of almost twenty-five years—my boss, my editor, my mentor, my lifeline to a new, out, second career. Steve gave me the opportunity to be a published author and, ultimately, a sit-down comic, breaking into show business at an age when I would more likely break a hip.

But it wasn't just my life he changed. He transformed the lives of so many of us here, in very different but monumental ways. By doing his daily work, at an organization he helped found, and dearly loved for more than a quarter of a century, he brought so many of us safety, freedom, amusement, respect, pride, friendship, legal protections, visibility, and an overall feeling of well-being you cannot underestimate.

Who else but Steve, in the early 1990s, could quietly confront an admittedly homophobic mayor—now this is two mayors ago—and turn him into one of our most ardent LGBTQ allies? Who else could have done that? Or seek out a tough as nails former police chief in a seriously homophobic town and turn him into a supporter and good friend?

Who else could see a bumper sticker saying *Keep Rehoboth a Family Town*, know the painful prejudice it represented, and answer with "I agree. Keep Rehoboth a Family town for all kinds of families."

Who else but Steve made certain CAMP Rehoboth participated in programs with the Library, Historical Society, Main Street or Chocolate Festival, making friends and allies of the very folks whose cars once wore those hateful bumper stickers.

Who else but Steve Elkins had the courage, as he fought for LGBT acceptance here, and this is so very important, to also call out our own community's occasional bad behavior and make sure we were living up to our good neighbor responsibilities?

In fact, he worked with the former police chief to start police and summer recruit sensitivity training for sexual orientation issues. At first it was tough, with the young men (and later, women) sitting stony faced, disinterested or sometimes even hostile.

"Who here knows any gay people?" Steve would ask. No one would raise a hand.

A couple of years in, Steve invited me to join those sessions and we heard some timid questions. "What do I do if people complain about two men holding hands on the boardwalk?" Steve explained to the young recruits that the guys were doing nothing illegal, and the complaining tourists were to be told that in a professional manner.

He asked the police to keep everyone safe and made sure we asked for no special treatment. Protect everyone and make sure everyone, gay or straight, upholds the law.

Each succeeding summer, those sessions lightened, and, by a dozen years in, we had a majority show of hands when the recruits were asked if they knew any gay or transgender people. And in one instance one of the summer recruits proudly came out as gay to his colleagues right then and there.

Of course, things were not always sunshine and Louie's pizza. Steve, Murray and the CAMP Board, staff and volunteers dealt with gay bashings on the boardwalk, the AIDS epidemic, helping to prevent HIV infections, tough financial issues for a fledgling nonprofit, and a frustrating lack LGBTQ legal protections.

Using CAMP Rehoboth's magazine *Letters*, which started as a two-page mimeographed bulletin and grew into a magazine of more than 100 pages in the summertime, Steve, as editor, made judgment call after judgment call about what CAMP should communicate to readers, even as it entertained.

And while Steve and Murray, along with the Founder's Circle and hundreds of others, built the community center, Steve was not one to stay upstairs in that cramped ivory tower. You'd see him taking out the trash, making sure the building was locked during his nightly dog walks, and trying to convince us to serve only light-colored beverages in the new Community Center.

That Steve was proud of the work he and Murray did to transform Rehoboth goes without saying. Year after year Steve sat backstage at the Sundance auction, with Murray's paintings, donated art, jewelry, and luxury cruises going for big bucks. Like clockwork, Steve would hide behind the sound equipment, smiling, but with tears of thanks streaming down his face.

Steve was honored to be asked to join Delaware's Human Relations Commission. He volunteered what little precious free time he had to hearing complaints and making decisions that changed people's lives for the better.

In 2013, Steve and Murray were awarded the rarely given *Order of the First State* for meritorious service to the State of Delaware, signed by Governor Jack Markell. The framed document hangs in a place of honor at their home.

And of course, between 2008 and now, Steve worked with so many legislators, volunteers, and advocates to provide us with LGBTQ anti-discrimination legislation, civil unions, and marriage equality.

It's great to wear the wedding rings and have the parties, but the legal protections Steve and Murray and others worked so hard to achieve are illustrated by one single astonishing sight. In the week following Steve's passing, in this once-divided hometown, flags at Rehoboth Beach City Hall and the police department flew at half-staff for this man. It was stunning in so many ways.

So yes, we get the legacy. But Steve had so much fun along the way. One time he heard an early morning radio rant about gay people writing nasty things on the walls at the old, lower-level Rehoboth Bandstand bathrooms.

He called me at 7 a.m. "Meet me there in fifteen minutes and we'll take a look."

He and I giggled that a *Gazette* photographer might catch the two of us going into the men's toilet together. "What would they make of that?" he laughed.

Well, down in that dingy space we did see several scrawlings on the walls. Nothing specifically gay, just garden variety nasty. The real surprise was then going into the ladies' room and finding, scrawled in there, much more explicit heterosexual commentary. We howled.

And, as many of you know, Steve looked fabulous in a pink tutu, had one of the best naughty smiles on the planet, and loved parading down Baltimore Avenue in his Follies costume as the Fruit of the Loom bunch of grapes. He adored feeling pretty and witty and gay.

Everyone thought the pink boa he wore for Broadwalk on the Boardwalk to fight Cancer was in honor of the day. It was. But also, in honor of Steve's love for wearing a pink feather boa. How we all wish he could march with the survivors next Sunday.

Steve gave everything he had to Murray, his family, his personal circle of friends, CAMP Rehoboth, and the community. I'm pretty sure Steve wanted me to end with some humor here, about Ru Paul, or Kinky Boots, but I cannot. I will miss him with every word I write. We will all miss him in our own ways but be ever grateful he was here to nurture such incredible love—look at you all! Incredible respect and truly amazing progress.

And although I could go on, I'm already well over Steve's strict 800-word limit for me. Any second, my editor for life will cut me off. So, rest in peace, my friend; you looked *mahvelous* in those hot pink feathers.

MARCH 2018

Back in the Saddle Again

Here at the magazine *Letters from CAMP*, we are mourning the loss of our fearless editorial leader Steve Elkins and I have since been tapped as interim editor of *Letters*. I cannot possibly fill his shoes, but I can put my editor's hat back on and return to work. It was a very short semi-retirement.

While I'm known in Rehoboth and environs as a writer, more than two decades ago, I left a job as managing editor of a community newspaper in Montgomery County, Maryland, to move to Rehoboth. Here, I could live, write, and enjoy an authentic life, out and proud.

But back in the day, writing columns for my newspaper job made a liar out of me. Deep in the closet in the 1980s and '90s, I had to write my stories without referring to the other person involved or, worse, changing pronouns. My wife Bonnie was a dangling participle. It was painful.

And, in those days, even when I wrote some of my humor columns for the *Washington Blade*, I had to use a silly pen name lest my boss learn the truth and, quite possibly, fire me. That was a real and scary possibility.

In 1995, when I started sharing stories in *Letters*, I could be honest, candid. Everything was true. It was glorious. So, in 1999, I quit my job and moved to Rehoboth, never looking back.

Now I'm looking back because I'm in the editor's chair again. I have to say, a lot has changed since I worked for *The Montgomery Village News* (1982-1999) and *Gaithersburg Gazette* (1980-81). For one thing, we have computers and the cloud. Yes, I'm so old that we used to put our newspapers together by cutting and pasting and using a hot wax machine (Ow! Ow!) to stick stories into layouts.

We used to go to a production house to lay out and paste-up each issue, sharing space with other publications. I remember one time when the layout room was occupied by our *Village News*, along with the president of the Washington, DC, chapter of PFLAG putting together his newspaper, and an editor pasting up a publication for a rabidly conservative political organization.

It was during the 1992 presidential primary season, and the PFLAG paper and the conservative paper had dueling stories about gay rights. One was pro, one was con, and it was very ugly in the room that day as a loud name-calling debate broke out, and we had to separate the battling editors.

I certainly don't expect any shouting or fisticuffs around our current *Letters* production. After all, paste-up and hot wax have been traded for computers and a talented layout team. And while thirty years have seen great progress in both gay rights and respect for our community, I'm pretty sure there are still publications (print and online) spewing hateful rhetoric. Luckily, we no longer need to share space with them.

I'm sad for the reason I'm back in the saddle, but happy to have my editor's hat on again, at least for a little while. That's me, aging in place in front of my computer. No hot wax in sight. Who needs retirement, right?

APRIL 2018

For the Love of Stuff

Downsizing to a smaller home is hell. Whether you are doing it for yourself, or for a parent, it's much like a colonoscopy.

You get rid of a lot of crap. But unlike the medical procedure, downsizing takes longer to complete and after eleven trips to Goodwill or the dump, you're too tired to go for a nice lunch.

My stepmother is moving, and my spouse and I spent a lost weekend picking through decades of accumulated possessions to decide exactly what goes to Florida.

First, let me say, I love my stepmother. My bio-mom passed away when I was twenty, and my stepmom took the job forty-five years ago. She's seen me through a lot over the years and might just be my favorite relative.

That being said, here's all you really need to know about her: She once took an assertiveness training course and didn't like it, but was afraid to quit. Decisions are not her strong point.

Which brings us to the kitchen. Or the garage. Or the linen closet. Mom is an exquisitely neat hoarder. Nothing like the rooms of debris you see on television, this house is meticulously tidy, showing gorgeously for real estate agents. But it's chocked so full of carefully stashed paraphernalia that finding one deviled-egg plate of the three she owns, or the octagonal, not round tablecloth embroidered by *her* grandmother amid dozens of others requires Google maps.

Her clothes closet contains outfits older than her fifty-eight-year-old biological son.

There is stuff packed so deep in the closet, it rivals where I was when I first met my stepmom.

And for the record, perhaps in reaction to visiting a home with twelve sizes of ramekins, eighteen cut glass decanters, and a stack of long-playing records and cassette tapes without devices to play them on, I own exactly one tablecloth and no plates exclusively to display halved hard-boiled eggs.

So last weekend, as we tried to elicit decisions about how many of the seventy-four cookbooks Mom actually uses and whether or not just one weighty iron frying pan, not four, will suffice, we saw the *New York Times*. It ran a feature on Marie Kondo, author of "The Life-Changing Magic of Tidying Up," which has sold 6 million copies.

The book includes something called a "once-in-a-lifetime tidying marathon." We were already 5K into it. Who knew?

The marathon requires sorting clothing, books, papers, miscellaneous and sentimental items, looking at each thing one at a time and determining if it makes you joyful. If not, it goes away.

We sat at the kitchen table, sipping coffee from the newest of mom's three kinds of coffee pots, served in one of her twenty-seven mugs and vowed to use the system.

By noon we were on decision six, stopped in our tracks by a 1960s era mink coat she won't wear because animal activists will throw red paint on it.

I thought the coat closet would be easy, there being no need in Florida for three Vortex winter parkas, a 1970s camel hair coat, two fleece-lined squall jackets, and dozens of hats and gloves. Not to mention the mink. "But what if I visit in the winter?" Mercy.

We got Mom to admit to no joy in the rusty movie screen for Super 8 movies and slides now safely on a DVD. Ditto seven kinked hoses, two rusty beach chairs, a broken microwave, three dented file cabinets filled with stray parts from long-gone appliances, a non-transferrable home health care potty chair, and a pull-along shopping cart last used by a little old lady in Brooklyn in the 1940s.

Not to mention a shopping bag with every plastic bag from

newspaper delivery for the last fifteen or twenty years. What, in case she got a dog?

Now there's something existentially disturbing about paying money at the dump to discard stuff you paid good money for in the first place. But I have to say, laughing and chucking years of useless junk into big dumpsters was kinda freeing and fun. Wheeee!

Back home we showed mom how to get recipes from the internet, then schlepped all but twelve of the cookbooks to the library for donation. I solved the mink coat dilemma. I said I knew a drag queen for whom it would bring joy. That worked.

Then we discovered our best trick yet. When pointing to certain stuff, Mom would ask if we liked it and if we'd like to have it. We said, "We'd love it!" to everything even close to being useful and wound up with a car crammed with stuff she could live without if she knew somebody else was hoarding it. Progress.

We almost had to hire a Bekins van to get home, the SUV looking like *The Beverly Hillbillies* in transit, right down to the chair strapped to the roof.

The moving truck comes to Mom's house this week. Our yard sale is Saturday.

This is the only kind of marathon I'll ever compete in. And it made Mom and a drag queen happy. What could be better?

MAY 2018

Not a Spitting Chance

Okay, I'm about to spit into a tube and mail my saliva to Utah.

As a result, many weeks from now, Ancestry.com is going to tell me my genetic heritage. I don't expect any surprises, as I'm pretty sure I'm the product of Eastern European Jews who emigrated to the US in the late nineteenth or early twentieth century.

But I'm not sure. I know my mother's parents came here as children; I think my father's parents were born here. I say I think, because in the 1950s, '60s, and even early '70s, when my family and I might have been discussing these things, nobody ever talked about it.

Assimilation was key, the past was past, and after World War II, many people wanted to distance themselves from their heritage, staying closeted, as it were. My father, an ad man on New York's Madison Avenue worked with many men who changed their names to avoid still-rampant anti-Semitism. My father did not change his name, but neither he nor his parents ever discussed a word about their heritage or history.

On my mother's side, I heard only two tales. The first was how my mother, daughter of Jewish immigrants, came to have the Irish maiden's name Kelsey. "When our family came to this country, the immigration clerk couldn't pronounce my grandfather's name Onakelski so he scribbled "Kelsey" on the immigration form. That's her story, and she stuck to it.

The second story surfaced years later, just before my Aunt Marion, the last of her generation, passed away. I told her I'd visited Ellis Island, saying "I felt close to my roots." She answered, "Didn't you know, dear, we came in illegally through Canada." Nope, didn't know. Seems I'm barely three generations removed from the DACA program.

Like many people, I learned of the immigrant experience from movies, books, history class, and politics. The only personal thing on my father's side was meeting my Great, Great Uncle Leo when I was six. My dad pointed him out, noting "That's Leo; he fought in World War I—on the wrong side." I had no clue what he was talking about, but I pictured Uncle Leo on a horse, wearing one of those black helmets with the pointy brass thingie on top.

So, sadly, by the time genetics drove the popularity of genealogy, there were no family elders left to question.

It was two weeks ago when Bonnie saw on ad on TV for Ancestry.com, offering a sale on their spit-in-a-tube kits. Knowing how much I love a bargain, Bonnie suggested I send away for the packet for the spit test. So I did.

While awaiting its arrival, I read that hidden in the output from unsuspecting spitters might be information to nab a murderer, like the solving of the "Golden State Killer case." I don't think I need worry about unearthing a family serial killer—serial scofflaws with unpaid NYC parking tickets, maybe.

Likewise, I've been warned that my DNA could unearth paternity surprises. It would be grand if my DNA tapped me as Rothschild progeny, but with my luck I'd come up related to Bernie Madoff.

So, the little box arrived, I signed on to Ancestry.com to register my collection tube and worked to produce a saliva sample. It's not as easy as you'd think. I needed several tries to collect enough liquid. And my spitting sounds were similar to what happens when I see POTUS on TV.

I also wondered if the sample remained tinged with happy hour's Grey Goose. Might it inadvertently reveal my relation to Russian potato farmers?

Nevertheless, I sealed up the tube and got it ready for mailing.

The final step in the process was checking the online box for *"I consent to the collection and processing of my DNA data and other sensitive Personal Information as described above."*

Puleeze. There really cannot be any sensitive personal information left for me to spill, having written about my life on these pages for twenty-five years, publishing most of it in five books since 2004. What's left to know?

As for the family tree Ancestry.com says I can fill out, the branch stops here. I can go back and add some ancestors, but from this point forward it's all schnauzers, all the time. Although it's very possible that Windsor had a distant relative who fought for the Germans in World War 1.

Now I just wait for the report about my ancestral origins, ethnicity estimate, and geographical subregion details. Honestly, I think my choice of dining at Rosenfeld's Deli or Lori's Oy Vey Café a couple of times a week tells pretty much the same tale my saliva will reveal. Here's hoping I find a long-lost cousin in the deli business or, better yet, an heir to the Stolichnaya vodka fortune.

Meanwhile, I wait. Just the offspring of illegal immigrants, paying my taxes, and being the nemesis of the GOP. I could just spit.

JUNE 2018

It's Pride Month and I'm Feeling It

On the first of June, the first day of Pride Month, it was time for our annual dog and pony show about the area's LGBTQ community with the seasonal park rangers from Cape Henlopen State Park.

CAMP Rehoboth has been doing this gig as part of the rangers' training for over twenty years now. For almost all those years, I've participated in the training with our late Executive Director, Steve Elkins. Over the years, we've seen many positive changes in the reception we've gotten, and in the whole attitude of the young rangers toward the relationship between law enforcement and the area's LGBT residents and visitors.

This June 1 session was spectacular. Following my short talk about CAMP Rehoboth, our community here, and what we expect from interactions with law enforcement (if we need help, help us; if we are disobeying regulations, cite us), the Q&A session sparkled.

Unlike years ago, where we were met with stony-faced silence, no questions and grudging attention, there was great interaction this time. These young people were familiar with LGBTQ issues and culture. Their questions showed respect and an eagerness to learn.

Q: "What's the most respectful way to address transgender men and women?"

A: Address them by "sir" or "ma'am," matching the way they are dressed and presenting to you.

Q: "How do I tell people complaining about two men holding hands, because they don't want their grandchild to see, that the men are doing nothing wrong?"

A: Um, exactly that way.

Likewise, we discussed what happens if LGBTQ people disobey regulations. We know that occasionally somebody thinks it's a good idea to hide in the dunes at North Shores for hanky-panky. I remember somebody coming into the CAMP Rehoboth office complaining about the rangers "targeting gays" for this activity.

"Well, that's illegal," they were told. Gay or straight, they *should* cite you for that. We must be good neighbors. CAMP and the Park Police commanders have always made sure the "targeting" was for bad behavior, not sexual orientation.

It's a happy Pride month when we can see such progress.

Of course, the Trump White House has proclaimed June to be, among other things, National Homeownership Month, National Ocean Month and Great Outdoors Month. Now I appreciate all that as I own a home near the ocean, and occasionally experience the great outdoors. But there has been no proclamation of National Pride Month as there was between 2009 and 2016. Who's surprised?

Since taking office, the president has proposed the transgender military ban, overseen the disappearance of the mention of LGBTQ citizens from several federal website pages, disbanded the President's Advisory Council on HIV/AIDS, and picked Mike Pompeo—a man who reiterated his disagreement with marriage equality at his confirmation hearing—to be Secretary of State. Oh, and the president's choice to head the Centers for Disease Control and Prevention is Dr. Robert Redfield, who has long been affiliated with a group claiming God punished gays with AIDS. Nice.

Now I don't know about everyone reading this magazine, but I certainly am proud of all the folks working to register voters and speaking out about electing a more gay-friendly (not to mention kinder, more sensible) Congress. We want legislators who will not only give us the symbolic boost of proclaiming Pride Month but, more importantly, work for—not against—our LGBTQ community. I won't stop working or speaking out until the White House is once again lit up with rainbow colors. Now that would make me proud.

Hey, White House, we don't need no stinkin' Pride Month from you. We proclaim our own!

JULY 2018

Slots of Fun

The last time I visited Las Vegas was the day Richard Nixon resigned and nobody in the hotel noticed. So, it's been a while. But the more things change the more Las Vegas stays the same—a garish, 24/7 adult amusement park. I was secretly hoping for history to repeat itself with another presidential resignation, but no such luck—with that, or anything else Vegas-related.

The hotels have gone from ginormous to gargantuan, and every celebrity chef not caught up in the #MeToo movement is there searing steaks you can't afford to eat. The casinos still have no windows or clocks. While the urban myth that casinos pump extra oxygen into the atmosphere to keep you awake and gambling longer has been debunked, some cosmic force kept me feeding Hamiltons into oblivion longer than good sense should have allowed.

There have, of course, been improvements in the slot machine industry in the forty-four years since I last donated money to Wayne Newtonland. Everything is digital now, and casinos use theatrics to replicate the authentic slot machine experience. Gone are the buckets of nickels that once made us giddy and turned our palms filthy. Now, when you cash out, you get ear-splitting sound effects of nickels cascading into a nonexistent cup while a dreary paper receipt prints out. Way less satisfying.

And the one-armed bandits no longer have any arms at all. Their levers have been replaced by neon buttons, each bet requiring absolutely no physical exertion. Gone is the illusion of losing weight along with your lunch money. I did find a retro machine, watched it gobble my ten-dollar bill, and pulled the handle. If not for the cacophony of casino bells and whistles, everybody would have heard me scream. The bandit's arm was a phony, and I almost dislocated my shoulder.

I was amused, however, by the new-fangled slot machine games. No longer mere cherries, bars, and 7s, the digital animations present all animals great and small, tempting pots of gold, flying honeybees, monsters, and Kung-Fu legends. Jurassic World dinosaurs in vivid 3D performed like a seizure starter kit.

Just like a lot of things these days, the distractions served to cover up what was really going on. I was losing, although these new machines seemed to toy with me longer before swallowing my moolah.

Eventually, I cut my losses and took a chance on the outdoors. And because global warming is a myth, it was 115 degrees out. Sure, you can give me that "it's a dry heat" bull-puckey, but I got second-degree burns grabbing a hot metal handrail. I should have packed oven mitts.

Once outside and gasping for air, all I had to do was whip across a footbridge above the famed Strip and enter another colossal hotel. I have to hand it to the architects and designers. Each hotel is more over the top than the next.

Truly, the buildings, inside and out, are works of art. I could have saved a lot of dough last winter, skipped Italy, and just visited Vegas. Who knew Venice's Grand Canal, complete with gondolas and serenading gondoliers, runs right through the Venetian Hotel lobby?

When I go to Paris, France, in two weeks I'll have no need to ascend the Eiffel Tower. Been there, did that at the Las Vegas Paris Hotel. It's only half the size of the Parisian attraction, but from the top, the bright lights of The Strip proved *tres magnifique*.

And ye gods! At Caesar's Palace there are gods all over the place, ancient ruins, Ionic columns, and The Three Graces in the flesh. Well, plaster. It really is big, bold, cheesy fun.

Later, I joined a group of friends for a ride on a giant pod Ferris Wheel. The half-hour journey had us rise high above the concrete jungle and desert floor as we gaped at surrounding mountains and the ridiculousness that is Las Vegas. We could see a Lawrence of Arabia dust storm brewing to the west and a lightning storm threatening from the east. It was a little scary, but impressive as hell.

Truth is, my Vegas weekend also included a literary conference, providing a modicum of quiet and culture for at least part of my stay. I also sampled my first In-N-Out Burger, which I believe bests Five Guys.

Then I prepared to take my first red-eye flight home. By the time I dragged myself to the airport, the only thing to keep me upright before boarding was to play more slots. Yes, they are at every single airport gate.

I played Pompeii Times and got snuffed out. In the DaVinci Painting Game I was Mona Loser. The 101 Dalmatian Chase saw my money go up in smoke. And Quack Pot, with spinning ducklings, made me giggle as another six bucks stayed in the local economy.

I'm home now. What happens in Vegas stays on your credit card.

JULY 2018

Drinks Well with Others...

As you may know by now, this can be a pretty self-deprecating column. I really haven't held back on reporting about any of the ridiculous fixes I've been in, or the idiotic adventures Bonnie and I have accidentally or willingly experienced.

Until now.

I've kept a cone of silence on the following twin stories for several months now for fear that what's left of our reputations would be shot, even after appearing ridiculously in these pages for the last twenty-three—count 'em, twenty-three—years.

But truth be told, the ugly truth must be told. When you think of this column, and you will, be kind.

The tales involve the same pair of guys who have been a bad influence but wonderful friends to us for over two decades of good times. And to be fair, in our long, speckled history together, this is the first incident to produce actual bodily harm.

Several months ago, we spent a long happy evening bar hopping, and as is wont to happen, every time Bonnie or I turned our heads a fresh Mojito or glass of Scotch would magically appear. I confess, we knowingly drank them. And laughed, traveled from Parrot to Pond, then wound up at Confucius, where I think hot Sake was involved.

While Ubering back to the boys' house, Bonnie "sleepily" leaned against the backseat door. Upon arrival, chivalry had not died, and one of the guys ran around to open the door. And Bonnie fell out, taking down her boyfriend and landing heavily on her own hand under her own butt. They wallowed on the ground just long enough for neighbors to drive by and embarrass everyone involved.

Surgery for Bonnie's torn hand ligament was required.

Swearing off Johnny Walker with Sake chaser, recommended. Tossing it off to being a klutz, without publicizing the details, the better part of valor.

Oddly, it was only a short time later I got my turn in the limelight. Only it was more like the lime garnish. It was during those sad, dark days last April as I prepared for a memorial service for a dear friend. I was clearly a mess, so to cheer me up, my very same pals escorted me to the Blue Moon, while Bonnie ran sound for a show at CAMP Rehoboth. And if you've ever had one Cosmo at the Moon, you know you'd best not have two. Perhaps it was three.

Wisely noting I needed food, the boys hustled me to the Pond, where we waited for my carryout chicken wings. Apparently, in the interim, this old, married lesbian gave unsolicited marital advice to a whole bachelorette party of fresh-faced young women. It was reported that I got applause. Perhaps for going away.

Then my friends called George the Taxi, who ferried me home.

Since Bonnie had our keys, I unsteadily walked to our hidden key stash, bent for retrieval, toppled over and began rolling downhill toward my neighbors' house. Righting myself onto all fours, I crawled back to the key crevice thinking "thank God, nobody can see me."

George could. Not only was he watching to make sure I got into the house, but he was also reporting everything on an open phone line to the boys at the Pond. "She's getting the key, oh my, she's down, she's rolling, she's on her hands and knees, she's back up, she's down again . . ."

All this, on speakerphone, live at the Pond.

For the record, I got into the house, suffered only grass stains, and woke up without a hangover. No one had the balls to tell me about George's broadcast or my playing Dear Abby to the bachelorettes for a week.

But I'll tell you this, the two episodes left us shaken, not stirred.

Because no matter how many photos I've taken posing with or swilling Cosmos, or how many jokes there are in my show about Bloody Marys or Grey Goose, I'm not really a heavy drinker (well, I'm heavy, but the drinks aren't). In fact, I haven't had a real hangover since 1972.

And while Bonnie loves her New Orleans T-shirt that says Drinks Well with Others, it's not an indicator of anything dire. Sure, we love happy and yappy hours, and enjoy a cocktail when out on the town, but not so much that it's the talk of the town. The only rehab we're eligible for is addiction to Louie's toasted grinders.

So, yes, we admit to being absolutely horrified by our recent outrageous behavior. And yet, given the number of birthdays amassed between us, we are also quite proud that we see no good reason to act our age.

Bottoms up. And that's the whole truth and nothing but.

AUGUST 2018

Ooh La La! Something I'll Never Forget

The Tenth Gay Games in Paris, the week of August 4, was an experience magnifique!

My dream of walking into the stadium with our eight-member Team Rehoboth for the opening ceremonies was just as sweet as I envisioned and twice as emotional.

The Games happen every four years, and this was the tenth edition of the games, which started in San Francisco forty years ago when gay athletes faced discrimination in the Olympics.

For the 2018 opening ceremonies, the US marched in early, and Delaware lined up right behind California. Seven of us waited to enter, as our eighth teammate (and captain), Bill McManus, marched in earlier as a board member for the Federation of Gay Games.

As we peeked from the entry tunnel, the crowd of thousands seemed small in a stadium for 50,000, but it had to be 10,000, with the lion's share of athletes still to enter and take their seats. The crowd cheered, hollered, and "did the wave."

As we set foot on the field, two French hosts preceded us, waving a Delaware placard and announcing "De La Ware" over the thundering loudspeakers.

Behind us, Florida and Georgia stood ready, followed by the rest of the states, and countries from Albania to Zambia.

As we started to cross the field, hundreds of thoughts collided in my brain, most echoing some form of "we're queer, we're here, and this old dame can't really believe it." I'm pretty sure those rioting queens at Stonewall couldn't have envisioned the glory of this moment, either.

I held the left side of the rainbow Team Rehoboth banner, my friend Anne Geary held the right, and in between stood

David Nelson, Bruce Robertson, Glen Parr, and Joe Della Torre, with Bonnie frolicking behind us, cheering and punching the hot night air with her fist. We crossed the center of the field, grinning, whooping it up, and feeling various blends of pride, thankfulness, and the need for another cold brew.

We'd been lining up in the brutally hot sun for hours, visiting other delegations and joining the crowd in guzzling so much beer the vendors ran out.

We soaked up every delicious hoot, holler, and moment.

As we ended our cross-field journey and scrambled to seats, teams continued the march in for almost an hour and a half, filling the stadium to at least 15,000 people, with enormous contingents from the likes of the UK (900) and Germany (700), and finishing with thousands of French participants.

In between there were teams of every size, including many brave individuals from places where it is both illegal and dangerous to be queer and here. There were two athletes from Jamaica, only one from Macau, several from Papua New Guinea, and, oddly, more gay athletes from Uganda than Rehoboth. I couldn't stop thinking about what many of them risked just to show up.

Denmark, Israel, Italy, Norway, Surinam, Switzerland— just overwhelming. Of course, there were costumes. Texas had cowboy hats, Thailand wore towering Buddha-like headdresses, Mexico had musicians camping it up, and the Chinese team tossed adorable toy pandas into the air.

The ceremony included song, dance, and Cirque du Soleil-style acrobats. When the stadium jumbotrons lit up with the words "We are stronger together," everyone watching knew it to be true.

The next day, the Athletes' Village came to life at Paris City Hall, with vendors, sponsors, entertainment, and food trucks. The enormous, architecturally impressive, and historic L'Hotel de Ville, dating back well before the French Revolution, stood draped in twenty-first-century rainbow banners.

Rue des Archives, in the Marais District Gayborhood, simply exploded with rainbow flags, crosswalks, Gay Games banners, and glitter. Men and women filled the establishments, spilling into the streets, a jumble of ages, languages, and attire. It was Gay Paree indeed.

Throughout the week, Bill, David, and Bruce bowled; Bonnie and Anne golfed; Glen and Anne half-marathoned; and Joe and I "coached." And everybody got souvenir participation medals.

I might add, we did not go hungry or thirsty throughout the week either, but that's a whole other kettle of fish, pate, red wine, and croissants.

I would be remiss not to mention the giant dance parties, including the massive Women's Party hosted by our friends at Olivia Travel. It was held aboard a humongous barge docked along the banks of the River Seine. Despite dozens and dozens of countries represented, the music was so loud no one could hear the diversity of language, so it looked and felt just like a giant tea dance at home. Only with better scenery and a younger demographic.

Not that there weren't some old gals there like me. There were. And we were the only ones who printed our tickets out on paper instead of waving our iPhones around for entry.

So, August 3-9, I came, saw, and even conquered a plate of snails. Seriously, clutching my part of that banner, representing Rehoboth in the International Gay Games, and having this experience is something still hard for me to realize ever could and ever did actually happen. And it's surely something I will never ever forget. Along with those snails.

AUGUST 2018

Avez Vous Any Ice?

Bonnie and I just blew out our travel budget with two weeks in France and Switzerland following our week at the Paris Gay Games. Next summer we get to travel to Millsboro.

Instead of my writing about the magnificent sights, here are some insights we gleaned.

In big cities, like Paris and Geneva, hundreds of grown men in business suits commute on teeny tiny stand-up scooters like we rode in our toddlerhoods. It's a bit oxymoronic.

Europeans don't understand ice. For the most part they make awful cocktails and serve them and soft drinks lukewarm with one or two small cubes at most. Water is served only slightly chilled. Since it was over 95 degrees for most of the trip, we resorted to guzzling ice-cold beer *every single day*—once, at a late breakfast. Beer saved our hydration levels and our vacation. We're now doing caloric penance.

In the Alps, even without a fear of heights, you'll reconsider by the time you get up to the Mont Blanc viewing platform via two cable cars, an elevator, and a set of daunting metal steps. Then you step out onto the glass floor of a two-person glass cube, suspended in mid-air over snowy pointy peaks. Gorgeously unnerving.

We'd have spent more time up top but started suffering hypoxia, described on a warning sign as trouble breathing and, from lack of oxygen, decreased brain activity. These days I can't afford a decrease.

By the way, immediately after descending from our scary sunrise adventure, we had that breakfast beer. Between the deep freeze up top at 12,600 feet and global warming on the ground, I'd never been so cold and so hot on the same day.

A Mont Blanc pen purchase was out as it cost almost as much as the vacation.

In Geneva, Switzerland, it's all-time pieces all the time with literally thousands of shops with windows full of absurdly expensive wristwatches. Neon signs shine atop skyscrapers, reading Rolex, Patek Philippe, TAG Heuer, Tissot, and even Swatch. Nobody has to ask anybody for the time.

Also in Geneva, the owner of a charming little restaurant asked, "What state are you from?" We said "Delaware," expecting a blank look, but he said "Ahhh, tax shelters!" Our reputation precedes us.

Arriving in Zermatt in late afternoon with plans to leave early the next morning, we rushed to a cable car for our only chance to see the Matterhorn. But billowing clouds completely shrouded the famed peak. An hour later, after checking into our boutique hotel room (a synonym for boutique is minuscule) we stepped out onto the tiny balcony and there it was, a cloudless, stunning Matterhorn. We hit the minibar, then sat and savored the view.

In all the small towns, and some larger cities, you could easily make a film spanning several centuries without having to cover up any signs of contemporary life. I'm sure inside the houses there were computers, fifty-five-inch TVs and Roombas, but other than moving a few late-model Audis, BMWs, and satellite dishes, all the exteriors remain historically intact. No vinyl siding anywhere.

Did you know there are more than sixty miles of champagne cellars (Mumm, Veuve Cliquot, Tattinger, Pommery, and lots more) weaving their way under the city of Reims? Excavated in the 1700s for building material for the city, the resulting caves have been producing champagne for three centuries. The caves also served as hospitals, schools, and housing during the relentless bombing by the Germans in both world wars.

We toured, tasted, and learned that the Veuve in Cliquot

means "widow" and the veuve Cliquot, in 1805, at age twenty-seven, was the first woman to take over operation of a major champagne house. I'll drink to that.

We took comfortable trains through the Alps, laughing, holding onto our sliding wine glasses in the dining car as we headed steeply up or down mountains. We drove from the Alps back to flatter terrain in Dijon ("Have you any Grey Poupon?") with Bonnie handling the ridiculously twisting, switchback roads like a NASCAR driver.

And then there were the dogs, absolutely everywhere, including dining with us inside most restaurants. We ate Gruyere cheese fondue in the town of Gruyere; photographed the Paris house where Gertrude Stein and Alice B. Toklas lived; ate chocolate croissants, baguettes, and crepes to die for. Also, snails. And a ton of cheese. I could go on ...

But we were happy to come home to our much-missed dog, a mountain of ice in our Cokes, well-mixed drinks, and our boutique-like manufactured home with its vinyl siding. Oh, and the best Sundance weekend EVER.

But I kinda miss the excuse for having a guilt-free cold brewski.

SEPTEMBER 2018

The Final Straw

For me, it was the final straw. While I've been dutifully recycling my trailer trash for years, the story about the straws woke me up. When I heard that in the US alone, we go through 500,000,000 (million!) plastic straws a day, only to have them wind up in our landfills and oceans, I flipped out. No more straws for me. I'm going to have to suck it up a different way.

Now, I try to catch restaurant waitstaff before they robotically stick a straw in my drink. I've become a No-Straw zealot.

Yesterday my spouse and I stopped at Wawa for my strawless, ergo lidless, iced coffee. We're back on the road, and naturally, just as I lift the cup to my mouth, a driver ahead short-stops, sending a tsunami of Jungle Java up my nose and down my clothes. Dripping in decaf, snorting coffee, I visualize the planet I'm saving.

At home, plastic bags are forbidden, for they too bulk up landfills with non-biodegradable goop. So, I only use reusable supermarket totes. That is, if I remember to bring them from the car and into the store. Acme needs flashing neon signs in the parking lot warning us to bring our bags into the store.

Sometimes I remember my bags halfway between the car and the store and double back, waving off drivers who think I'm leaving and want my parking space. But most times I've shopped till I've about dropped, cart full of ice cream and other perishables when I realize my error. Hell, that's when I just buy another four reusable bags and rationalize that the money I'm losing is for the planet I'm saving.

I now have so many reusable grocery bags piled up my vehicle it looks like I'm living in the car. That is, if I remember to take the stacks of bags back to the car after unloading the groceries. I have so many reusable bags piled on a chair by my front door visitors think It's my laundry hamper.

And how about plastic water bottles? Literally billions are made, sold, and purchased annually only to have a small percent of them recycled, the rest spending eternity in landfills. Meanwhile, the internet shrieks about our ingesting radically free plastic particles, contracting dread diseases, poisoning mahi-mahi and destroying our environment. So naturally, I spurn bottled water.

Now I carry my own reusable flasks filled with Rehoboth's finest tap water. That is, if I remember to take the bottle from home. Most times I wind up finishing a walk or a day of power shopping parched, tongue hanging out like my dog. In fact, I've been known to buy bottled water specifically *for* my schnauzer. He should not suffer for my short-term memory loss. Or my crusade.

Coffee at home is problematic too. I love my Keurig single-cup maker, but it pains me to trash the used plastic K-cups. I bought a refillable little pod and when spooning coffee into them, spent more time wiping Pike Place Roast off the counters and out of my kitchen drawers than drinking the coffee. I crunched when walking from two tablespoons of course-grind Maxwell House in my sandals.

So, I bought recyclable cloth pods. After brewing, you peel the cardboard cover off, squeeze the coffee grounds into the trash and send the leftover pod to recycling. The meticulous act of peeling the pod away from the Dunkin' Original Blend left me with coffee grounds under my fingernails, a mess on the floor, and the threat of losing my mind while saving my planet. Also, by then it was lunchtime.

In addition, as casual recyclers, most of us never worried about snippets of food stuck to tins or leftover sludge in the bottom of a jar. But now I've learned that it's a big no-no. Now we have to scrub all jars, bottles, and tins clean before we flip them into the recycling bin.

I've always hated prewashing the dishes before putting them in the dishwasher, but now I get to scrub the recyclables too. How does this match recycling's mantra of Reduce, Reuse, Recycle if I'm wasting water and personal energy? And I could do a whole article on trying to rinse a mayonnaise jar. Water and Mayo don't mix, creating clots of white goo. Do this before lunch and it's better than Weight Watchers.

But despite the challenges I remain committed to it all. I'm still shouting, "Straws suck!" I'm boycotting plastic bags and happily driving knee-deep in reusables. I've started leaving my tote bags and favorite water bottle at the front door to remind me to take them along. Tripping on them and breaking an ankle is possible, but I'm on a mission.

I'm still fully committed to doing my bit to save my planet. For me, it's the last straw. I wear iced coffee well.

OCTOBER 2018

I Flew at iFLY

Once again, my wife and I saw no good reason to act our age.

In celebration of Bonnie's last birthday of her sixties, she requested an iFLY experience at an indoor skydiving facility outside Baltimore.

I knew I'd be on the no-fly list since I'd sworn off jumping out of—or from—anything ever again, following my harrowing zipline adventure.

But as terrible luck would have it, the iFLY Adventure launches patrons from the bottom up, with 100 mile-per-hour wind power lifting fliers up, up, and away. Gone was my spectator-only excuse.

First, we shed jewelry, eyeglasses, and inhibitions to suit up in bulky full-body superhero outfits, helmets, goggles, and earplugs. Then we went to "flight school," with our instructor John, also dressed like Captain Marvel. He coached us to respond to hand signals to straighten our legs, make an X with our body or, heaven help us, relax.

The chin-up signal was deemed crucial. I've been told "chin up" before, but if I didn't heed and cheer up, I was not in danger of crashing to the net floor, where the wind would give me a complimentary colonoscopy.

Class dismissed; we waddled over to the three-story flying tube.

I watched Bonnie grip the doorway to the wind chamber and get sucked in, positioned face-down, held up at first by Spiderman, then flying free. I lip-read her "Holy crap!" as she twirled and floated up and down, based on whether her legs were out straight or slightly bent.

I smiled, enjoying her five minutes of abject glee, forgetting for a nanosecond I was next.

As she grabbed the doorway, ejecting herself from the tube, she said "That was so cool!"

"Your turn!" yelled Captain America.

Bonnie and I exchanged glances, translated either "In case I die, I love you," or "If I die, I'm blaming you." I moved to grab the doorway.

Good luck to this skinny dude tasked with holding all of me up until I could catch the wind beneath my wings.

Whoosh! I was swept up, belly down, arms flailing, legs akimbo, in a complete spread-eagle. Unfortunately, my mouth, as usual, was open, sending rivulets of spittle out and G-forced up into my helmet. And just like that, Batman let go and I was flying in a Category 5 tornado, heading for Oz, a flying monkey, chin up, legs extended, shoulders back, arms in front of me like Superman, Wonder Woman, one of the Incredibles.

Only I wasn't thinking those things. I was thinking omigod-my heart-is-gonna-stop, whose-idea-was-this-get-me-down-I'm-too-old-for-this.

For what seemed like an eternity, the sustained winds suspended me like a Boeing air bus, chin up, shoulders forward, eyes-watering, spit flying, and for one brief shining moment I think I liked it.

When time was up, I catapulted out the door and staggered to a seat. You could see the tracks of my tears. Tufts of my hair stuck up through the small holes in my helmet like a Venus Flytrap.

Full disclosure, Bonnie gleefully took flight twice more, once for her included second flight and then another round for *my* included second flight. Why push my luck or rotator cuffs?

Cheers to instructor John for keeping us afloat, safe, and feeling proud of ourselves. We asked if we were the oldest flyers he'd tutored and he said, "Hell, no. We've had eighty-eight-year-olds." Glad we didn't wait that long.

Quite pleased with ourselves, we drove back to the beach, laughing, high-fiving, and repeating our mantra: *You don't stop playing because you get old, you get old because you stop playing.* Superwomen, indeed.

The next morning, I could hardly get out of bed. My hips ached. I couldn't turn my neck to the right. And I had trouble lifting my coffee to my mouth. It was an Advil kind of day.

I fly, but not like I used to.

OCTOBER 2018

Press 3 for a Nervous Breakdown

Artificial Intelligence, which is supposed to make our lives easier, is actually making them harder.

I can't explain this conundrum except to say that machines are so smart these days they've conspired to make us do their work. Take my groceries. Please.

The smart registers have convinced us to weigh our own cucumbers, scan all our groceries and bag them ourselves so there's nobody to curse out later when the chips are in crumbles. How is this easier than waiting a minute in line for a human, who needs a paycheck, to do all this?

And the more the machines know, the more I have to know. I never cared what kind of tomatoes I was buying. The cashier knew. I was lucky I knew they grew outside. Now I have to be sure to put the right tag on the Heirlooms.

And robots have ruined the airport. Last summer on our way to France I was directed to a nifty baggage-weighing robot by the lone employee at the check-in counter. He asked the machine do the baggage handling while he twiddled his thumbs.

I was dumbfounded by a robot that (or is it "who?") weighed my suitcase and spit out a baggage tag specific to my destination.

So instead of dragging my suitcase to the counter and picking it up only once before it flew to Paris, I had to schlepp it across the concourse to the robot, hoist it up on the scale, wait for smarty-pants to guess its weight, lift it off the scale, affix the baggage tag myself, then roll the damn thing back to the counter.

By this time there was a long line because a traveler up front had affixed the tag backward, increasing the likelihood of his never seeing his Samsonite again. Hopefully, in a few months the robot will have artificial limbs programmed to affix the tags correctly too.

When I finally got to the breathing person at the desk, he stood there, hands folded across his chest as I bench pressed my bag up once again, dumping it onto the conveyor belt, giving it a shove to get going, and praying Mr. Luggage Roomba had properly deduced where I was headed.

This is easier? For whom? Air France?

Then there's the original aggravating convenience of robotic telephone answering systems. All I wanted to do was let the bank know I was going overseas so they would approve my transactions there. It used to be easy. Call the number, press zero and you got an agent who made a notation and said "bon voyage."

Now, the artificially intelligent phone robot conducts an in-depth interview first. Prior to being connected to a human being, this was the exact conversation:

Please enter the last four digits of your card number.
Please enter your zip code.
Your balance is _____(a frightening number)
Your next minimum payment is_____(yipes!).
Your remaining credit is _____ (a number that rhymes with 'hero').
Your last payment of _____ was received on _____ (just under the wire).
If you would like to request a credit increase press one (Good god, no!).
If you wish to report a lost or stolen card press 2 (who wants to steal a maxed out card?).
To hear your reward balance press 3 (yippee, I can get two free Starbucks Macchiatos for spending my dog's inheritance).

At this point I suspected I'd be home from the Alps before

talking to somebody with a pulse.

To call about travel plans, press 4 (finally!).
But no, cruel joke. Pressing 4 I heard:
For a balance inquiry press 1.
For a new pin number press 2.
For travel plans . . . (YAY!!!) *press 3.*
Then comes "*Please enter the three-digit code on the back of your card.*" (AUUUGGGGHHHHH!!!!!)
"*Enter the first three letters of your mother's maiden name.* (Oh, for crap's sake)

What's next, blood type and Super G discount card?

Suffice it to say that when I finally checked in with a human I didn't even sound excited about the trip.

So, what's next for artificial intelligence? If robots really want to be helpful, they will hover around the house, telling me when leftovers become science projects, where I put my phone this time, and to please remember to put the reusable grocery bags back into the car.

For that matter the robot could take me shopping, remind me to bring the reusable bags into the store, tutor me on the difference between Heirloom and Brandywine tomatoes and stop me from trying to use the maxed-out credit card. A robot saving me from the humiliation of a card denied would be truly useful.

That'll be the day. Coming soon.

OCTOBER 2018

On My Honor, I Was Shocked

On Wednesday, September 26, I was given the wonderful privilege of being honored as the Girl Scouts of Chesapeake Bay's Sussex County Woman of Distinction for 2018. Here's what I had to say about this honor:

"Good afternoon. First, thank you all so much for being here. Not so much to honor me, although I really appreciate the support of all of you, but to help raise awareness of and funds for the really good work done by the Girl Scouts.

At ages five and eight, my younger sister and I were enrolled in ballet class. Within weeks, my sister showed incredible promise as a budding ballerina. Me, not so much. From the get-go I was perpetually a half step behind in the Hungarian Gypsy dance, and pitched a wild hissy fit, refusing to go onstage in a tutu.

My sister went on to a decade of dance, while my mother suggested I join the Brownies.

I loved it, flew up (that's what they called graduation) to become a Girl Scout, and was introduced to some of the things that would retain my interest and spark my career over a lifetime—like a photography badge. I would stalk my sister, parents, and the babysitter, and take frightening candids with my Kodak Brownie Starflash.

I learned about theater when we did a little play about Girl Scout founder Juliet Gordon

Low, who, by the way, was one tough cookie.

And speaking of cookies, *Death of a Salesman* had nothing on me. I once sold sixty-two boxes at a single Passover Seder. Good thing they were marked kosher. We saw the relatives less after that.

I wasn't really good with the outdoor stuff though. One time three other fifth graders and I sat squashed into the back, rear-facing seat of a 1958 Dodge station wagon. We each had a pad of paper and a pencil and, going for our Orienteering Badge, we drew a map of where we had just been. Pretty soon, all of us were nauseated from riding backward, and wound up sitting on the side of the road trying not to toss our Girl Scout cookies. I never got that badge, but I got a great candid photo of our troop leader with an expression that said, "Why me?"

Likewise, I forfeited the Outdoor Explorer badge when refusing to even look at a picture of a snake, much less risking an encounter with a real one. Bugs, too, were outside my wheelhouse, even as my scouting career reached into junior high school. As our troop leader explained the value of citronella as a mosquito deterrent, I announced that the best deterrent was staying in the house. The other scouts laughed; the leader did not.

And finally, as an adult, I want to know who thought it was a good idea to provide a pocketknife to an inquisitive eighth grader? Favoring the screwdriver function, at age twelve I went home and unscrewed every screw in the house, in many cases being unable to reassemble the toaster, table lamp, and my father's stereo record player cabinet. On my honor, I tried.

By the way, this pocket is so old it's in the Girl Scout Museum. Ouch.

So here I am, six decades later, a Girl Scout Woman of Distinction.

There are really two meanings to the word distinction. From Webster, the most common usage is "the quality or state of being distinguished or worthy." And for that I am truly honored for this designation and celebration.

The second, though, is "the act of perceiving someone or something as being not the same and often treating as separate or different."

I knew I was different from most of my friends at just about the same age I kicked that pink tutu across the room and ran off to join the Brownies. It took almost two more decades to define that difference and muster the nerve to come out of the closet as a gay woman.

From there, I continued to put to use the skills I honed throughout my Girl Scout youth. The lessons got me through high school and college, into journalism, theater, and activism, while still taking annoying candid photos. And hopefully, I've used my skills making a small difference, somehow for the better, in other people's lives.

And despite my failings in orienteering, camping, and stinkbug collection, I have been tapped for this honor by the Girl Scout organization.

It's been my privilege to be honored in the gay community for many things—my books, my fighting for equality, and my storytelling. It's been amazingly rewarding, and I am so grateful.

But on my honor, I swear, that I could never have imagined, all those closeted, fearful years ago, and even a decade ago, that the Girl Scouts, as progressive as they are, would celebrate a very openly gay person as their Woman of Distinction. I'm incredibly honored by this—for me, and for my community here in Sussex County. For this incredibly meaningful honor, I thank the Girl Scouts of Chesapeake Bay very, very much.

(shows antique Girl Scout pocket knife)
Anybody have a screw loose? I've got you covered."

NOVEMBER 2018

When in Rome

I have advice for you: travel while you can, my friends, when you are hardy, able to climb oodles of European steps and with sufficient lung power to do so.

I just got back from a ten-day tour of Italy and Mama Mia do my knees hurt. I wish I had trained for the marathon first. Both in stamina and wine consumption.

Seriously, those twelfth- century towns, not to mention the ancient ruins, were hilly as hell. And in places like Rome's colosseum, to get the full perspective on the gargantuan arena, we walked up a dozen stone flights to the top row where the peons used to sit. By that time, I myself was an ancient ruin.

We were told that the gladiators vowed fealty to the emperors, shouting "We who are about to die salute you!" Up on those battlements I was tempted to pledge that to our tour guide.

Later, a funny thing happened on the way to the Forum, literally. The monsoon-like rains came, with wind turning umbrellas inside out and water rushing ankle deep down the streets. "Pretend you are being splashed by chariots!" hollered our tour guide to his soaking wet charges. I am Spartacus and I am wet!!!!!

On the morning we arrived in Venice, the city was shrouded in a thick fog (I'd say pea soup but it was more pasta fagioli). There was so much cloud cover hovering outside our window we could have been overlooking Route 1. At street level, one false step and I'd be in the Grand Canal.

But soon it lifted, and we got to the business of walking up and down the 1,300 Venetian bridges, including the most famous, the Bridge of Sighs. After a day-long schlepp around town and through St. Mark's Square, dodging pigeons and souvenir hawkers, our group made myriad grunting noises that were a lot more vocal than mere sighs. But I have to say, the glorious Italian dinners and wonderful wines assuaged our ills.

In many Italian eateries, the wine comes with the meal, but you have to pay extra for water. My kind of deal.

On a trip to the Tuscan countryside, we visited a winery and fattoria. I've heard of a trattoria, but a fattoria? Is it what it sounds like? After our luncheon of antipasto, a generous slab of lasagna, crusty bread in olive oil, and decadent tiramisu for dessert, I was sure I understood. But no, a fattoria is a working farm where they press grapes into wine and olive oil. Who knew?

Then it was on to see the Leaning Tower of Pisa, which leans a lot more in person than in postcards. It looks perilous, and I refused to stand under the acute angle side. And yes, we tried to take those stupid pictures where you put up your hands to look like you are holding the building up. Love means never having to say you're embarrassed.

In Florence we made the obligatory visit to Michelangelo's David statue, and yes, it is unbelievably stunning in person. Even better were his unfinished statues, half-completed in blocks of marble, looking for all the world like people imprisoned in stone, trying to escape. Gorgeous.

We spent a long while admiring the magnificent ceiling in the Sistine Chapel, and all of us could have used a chiropractic adjustment afterward.

Also in Florence we walked and walked up and down elegant and unaffordable shopping areas, with window upon window of designer eyeglasses, shoes, and leather jackets costing more than our entire trip.

Many of the well-dressed, well-shod, perfectly coiffed men and women looked like extras right out of a James Bond movie. For one brief shining moment I was horrified by my Lower, Slower Delaware T-shirt and Nikes, but then I got over it.

And while we saw many iconic sights, ate, and drank like kings, and walked up and down every stone staircase in Italia, my favorite tourist mecca was the Trevi Fountain in Rome.

We saw it in the daytime, but decided to come back at night, when it was more romantic, to toss our coins.

Well, we could not find it again. Told it was walking distance from the hotel, we fired up Google Maps, then MapQuest, then Waze on my Smartphone and they all had conflicting distances and routes.

We walked and walked in circles, up and down those ridiculous Spanish Steps, and what seemed like up and down the seven hills of Rome for over an hour, and still couldn't find the damn thing.

How can you lose a fountain with twenty-foot rearing marble horses gushing water into a humongous pool? My kingdom for a Rand-McNally!

Romantic at night? By the time we finally staggered up to the fountain we were hardly speaking to each other.

But coins we did toss, romance filled the air, and we said arrivederci, Roma, with warm feelings for Italy, its awesome art, centuries of history, food, fattorias and fine wines.

But Dr. DeMille, I'm ready for my knee replacement now.

FEBRUARY 2019

Am I Queer?

Are you as sick as I am of listing the entire alphabet to refer to our community?

By the time I type LGBTQ+ I've forgotten the rest of the sentence. And readers are catching some ZZZZs as well.

So, am I just plain queer?

That's one solution proposed for replacing the current alphabet soup with a self-affirming umbrella term: calling us all queer. The *HuffPost* has a Queer Voices section, *Queer Eye* is back on TV, and the Urban Dictionary has tapped us all as one big Queer family.

Certainly, being simply queer is shorter and less complex. Quite descriptive, actually. And yes, all encompassing.

But is it comfortable? Nope. Calling myself queer gives me the yips, though I am trying hard to embrace it. Many in my generation probably agree, having grown up when being called queer was harrowing and hurtful. The word was often hurled at us in homeroom, at recess, or as we waited for the school bus, even before we ourselves knew we were, as was also the popular term at the time, homosexuals.

Whether out or closeted, we got called dykes and queers. Sometimes even faggots by clueless bullies ignorant of the proper gender slurs. And it was painful.

But, more than a half century ago (!), in the mid-1960s, prior to the 1969 Stonewall riots, our community started to usurp the lovely dictionary word "gay," turning its meaning from "a carefree person" to "a homosexual person."

What a great idea! It worked for me.

Once the Stonewall Inn erupted and newspapers and talk shows started coming to reluctant terms with the existence of homosexuals, there was lots of talk about gays. As a placard at the first Pride parade shouted, "Gay is Good!" And it was.

But the airwaves and newspapers mostly talked about gay men. People started seeing the term gay to mean men—mostly drag queens, leathermen, and, sadly, men dying of AIDS.

People hardly ever heard about gay women. And the word lesbian was seldom seen. Gay was good, but for the women it was the beginning of the long-standing lesbian invisibility crisis.

So smart lesbians everywhere set about correcting the record. The fight for the L word was on.

I remember being part of an argument, in the mid-1980s, with the editor of the *Washington Blade*—which, by the way, started life as the *Washington Gay Blade*. I was lobbying for inclusion of the word lesbian on the front page of the newspaper. It took lots of letters, conversations, and heated exchanges from a lot of women, but the L-word finally appeared under the *Washington Blade* banner. Victory! We had a newspaper for gays *and* lesbians.

What followed in quick succession was the rise of the L word, both as a common descriptor in communications and eventually on television with the brilliantly bitchy and beloved TV series of the same name.

So gays and lesbians were now more visible, but what about our bisexual and transgender brothers and sisters? We happily added them to the discussions, but by this point writing or saying gay, lesbian, bisexual, and transgender was becoming a bit of a mouthful, absolutely no pun intended.

Ergo, we got the shorter, snappier LGBT—yes, less specifically visible for each, but inclusive of all.

But it wasn't all. What about the young people who were questioning? Or those reclaiming the slur queer? Or intersex folks, or others wanting inclusion? That's how we first got LGBTQ+ and now it's a whole, dizzying list of letters. Try using LGBTQIAEIEIO in a sentence.

So, people are thinking we should get back to calling ourselves just plain queer. Of course, for some of us, it gives a flashback from the hate-strewn past.

A couple of years ago I went to a college campus to perform my show, *Aging Gracelessly: 50 Shades of Fay*. They gave me a large sign to post on my car's windshield so I wouldn't get a parking ticket. In big block letters it announced Queer Conference. I have to admit, seeing the word queer splashed across my windshield gave me the vapors.

But something has to be done. It's no longer possible to fit the whole laundry list of letters into a readable column, or effective conversation.

For my part, I wish we could just use the G-word, calling all of us gay. But if not, I will accept that we are all queer, we are all here, and everybody better get used to it. Me included.

So, call me what you want, but don't call me late for happy hour.

JANUARY 2019

Ah Yes, I Remember It Well

I sit, dumbfounded, in front of the computer, wondering what to do. How could I be hacked? I don't even know my own password, so how can somebody else know it?

Clearly, once again, this aging gracelessly thing is out of hand. My friends are getting emails from me recommending certain, um, marital aids. Do they still call them that? Is it now Dildos Are Us?

I couldn't change my password fast enough. Literally, I couldn't. My entire address book is continuing to receive solicitations for X-rated products. Yes, I am getting many snarky comments in return.

So, it seems my email password has been stolen. For the hell it's putting me through I should just change it to 666666.

The situation reminds me of an article I read giving awards for the very worst passwords of 2018. While mine didn't medal, I was not far off. The article celebrated the stupidity of passwords like "password" and "123456," while giving credit to the genius who marched across the top of the keyboard with "!@#$%^&*".

I love the guy who changed his password to "Incorrect" so when he got it wrong the site would tell him "Your password is Incorrect."

The article recounted the classics, like "I changed my password to BeefStew but was told it wasn't Stroganoff." Or the companion "I changed my password to fortnight but apparently that's two weeks."

So, here's my question. How come I can remember my convoluted nonsensical summer camp booster cheer more than, omigod, fifty-six years later, and I can't remember my #$%^& passwords. Or much of anything else for that matter.

But I forever recall:

> *Mahi, mahi, maho,*
> *A rumstick, a bumstick,*
> *A ninny-cat, a ninny-cat,*
> *So fat a rat.*
> *Hob-a-gobba rick-a-racka*
> *Hob-a gobba firecracker*
> *Hob-a-gobba razoo*
> *Johnny has a bazoo*
> *Siss-boom-bah*
> *My Camp, My Camp, Rah,*
> *Rah, Rah.*

I swear, this was never ever written down in my junior high Doodle Diary, on my Etch A Sketch, or in my spiral notebook. It was never memorialized on a day planner, IBM Selectric typewriter, word processor, or my first PC. Not on my Palm Pilot, BlackBerry or now, my bloody iPhone. NEVER. But there it stays, permanently imprinted in the back of my brain where my social security number should be.

I walk into the den and forget what I came for. But I know the *Mahi, Mahi, Maho.*

We order carry-out. "Hey, honey, which place had that steak sub you liked, Casapulla or Capriotti's?" *A rum stick, a bum stick,* I can't remember.

Did we say we'd meet up with pals on the boardwalk at Dolle's or up by the Henlopen? Damned if I know. I'm such *a ninny cat, a ninny cat.*

Hob-a-gobba ricka-racka is useless, but it's amazing how it surfaces more easily than the name of the woman across the room at happy hour. *Johnny has a bazoo* but I have no idea whether I have a dental appointment on Monday or Wednesday.

Wait a minute! By George, I've got it. At least as far as that interminable list of passwords is concerned. All I have to do is rotate the words to the *Mahi, Mahi, Maho* and I can crack my bank account, Xfinity, and facebook.

Hob-a-gobba firecracker, I'm on to something here. I can assign *Hob-a-gobba Firecracker* to Amazon, where I can buy everything including firecrackers. I can use *a ninny-cat, a ninny cat* for Windsor's Pet Health Insurance, *rumstick, a bumstick* for, let me think, hmmm... *bum stick*... my Health Insurance! Then it's just a short hop from *Siss-Boom Bah* to Ancestry.com and *Johnny has a bazoo* (think kazoo) to iTunes.

If I had an account with an exterminator, which I don't, I would certainly score with *so fat a rat.*

I don't know whether these passwords will qualify for the complexity or strength tests, need to be changed in 180 days or deter burglars, but hell, I can remember them. And maybe the hackers won't. After all, it's a far, far better thing I do, to make my passwords gibberish than to hawk adult sex toys.

Let's hear it for remedial computer security.

My brain, my brain, rah-rah-rah.

MARCH 2019

Snowbird Disaster

Over a year ago we rented and paid for an AirBnB dog-friendly rental for February 2019. With a friend planning to join us, and possible visitors, we selected a beautiful two-bedroom home with a convertible sofa and a small pool.

Just fourteen days before our arrival, AirBnB sent me a morning email. Subject: Craig Had to Cancel Because of an Emergency.

Apparently, he sold the house, making it an emergency only for us. Silly me, I thought a rental contract must be honored, but AirBnB said "NO," though they offered us a refund and $200 extra "to make sure you still have a great stay in Sarasota." Where? Sleeping in the bus station?

Thus, we began a frantic sixteen-hour computer siege, madly seeking shelter. Mind you this was when it was 13 degrees in Rehoboth and going home did not seem like a wise option. Or even a viable one, as we'd offered our home to a friend needing winter lodging.

Turns out AirBnB's $200 "gift" was solely for another AirBnB rental and there was absolutely bupkis available. Well, except for a $12,000-per-month beachfront Taj Mahal, but then March would be spent in debtor's prison.

We were screwed and in full-out homeless snowbird panic.

By 11 p.m., bleary-eyed and manic, I found a listing in an RV and manufactured home "resort." Okay. We've owned an RV, stayed in plenty of cool parks, and currently live in a very nice, manufactured home. Bring it on.

So, we quickly booked the two-bedroom (plus pull-out sofa) two-bathroom home. It was a little more expensive, but the park had amenities. On to Sarasota. How bad could it be?

OMG. We entered the park, driving by hundreds of RV sites and tiny manufactured homes so close together neighbors could easily watch each other's TVs.

Entering our property, our first impression screamed cluttered and ugly, mere months from an appearance on *Hoarders*. The décor would make a gay man weep.

As I could clearly see and hear the pontificating fiction reporters from FOX News on the fifty-five-inch screen next door, I studied our own "living room." With our TV mounted perpendicular to the couch, we'd have to watch MSNBC sitting shoulder to shoulder on the sofa with our heads permanently turned forty-five degrees to the right.

The skinny hallway led to a DIY project they called a bedroom but was merely an inside cabin barely the size of a bed. Beyond that lurked the purported half bath, a metal storage shed bolted to the trailer. All we saw was a toilet. It took us a good five minutes to find that a miniature sink sat perched atop the toilet tank. And get this—you turn on the faucet to flush. My god, I could multitask, straddling the toilet to pee, then stay in position to wash my hands.

Holy crap. The original rental cancellation was a disaster, but did that mean the remedy was a FEMA trailer?

The "master" had less than ten inches on either side of the bed to crabwalk in and out. I could not stand back far enough from the closet's sliding mirrored doors to see anything but my front teeth. I climbed onto the bed and stood up to see my pants.

House rules: no dogs up on the furniture unless you cover it with a blanket. There was already a dirty blanket on the sofa, which when removed revealed an even filthier fabric. We washed that blanket so *people* could be up on the furniture.

Moving along, we eyed the tiny "full bath" adjacent to the itsy-bitsy kitchen. If I faced the refrigerator to fill a glass from the icemaker, my backside was already halfway into the bathroom. Multitasking again.

And speaking of icemaker, the tiny table would have to double as a bar and my editorial office. Admittedly, having the Tito's so close as I typed would be mighty efficient.

And it was. Efficient and vital to survive. Which we did, barely. With our backs up against the wall in more ways than one, we made ourselves at home and had fun anyway.

The community amenities—pool, pickleball, and watercolor classes—provided the exercise yard to our cellblock. We ruled the phony half-bath off-limits except for emergencies. We dunked in the hot tub to soothe our TV-watching necks. And we braved hearing loss so the neighbors could fully appreciate Rachel Maddow. As added therapy we wrote a painfully honest and snarky online review of the overpriced horror house.

For this coming month we will be ensconced in a beautiful place in Gulfport, Florida. But heed our warning: AirBnBeware! Make sure you study the photos. Although in the listing, they didn't have the chutzpah to show the sink/toilet thingie. You can find one online. It's a gem.

APRIL 2019

Um... Stuff Happens

Over the past few years, as many of you may know, I've become known as a sit-down comic. A few weeks ago, though, I feared my career might be over.

I couldn't sit down. Or if I did, I couldn't stand back up. I was stuck at half mast, bent in half, screaming if I moved a muscle. It was a world-class lower back spasm.

Yes, here it comes. The Organ Recital, where we all talk about our medical problems.

I'm pretty sure I made the morning for the folks at the ER when the doc asked me how I hurt myself.

"I bent over to pick up dog poop."

Clearly a first for them, given their snorts.

When you're old, shit happens. Then you injure yourself picking it up.

And unlike my peers, this was not a pickleball injury with bragging rights, nor a softball hamstring pull with sympathy credit. No, I'd have to admit that this painful insult came from the grand sport of pooper scooping.

So, on the way home from the ER, prescriptions for extra-strength muscle relaxers and steroids in hand, we stopped at a Dunkin' Donuts, where my debit card was declined. Ah, shit continues to happen.

As Bonnie forked over six dollars in cash, my phone pinged. It was M&T Bank alerting me that they had just stopped a suspicious hot drink at Dunkin' Donuts. Seriously? Grand theft coffee? Did they think I was violating my diet?

Why weren't they suspicious the day before when I put wood screws and spackle on my credit card? For me, that was truly suspicious. But coffee and Bavarian Creme?

We did a drive-by at the pharmacy and I came home, popped pills, and made unattractive noises attempting to stand or sit down at regular intervals. I prepped for the evening ahead when, jacked up on steroids, I'd have time to read the complete Tolstoy in lieu of sleep. Or write my next eleven columns for this magazine.

As the steroid mania kicked in, my speeding brain thought it was a good idea to call the bank and ask why they saved me from donuts. I was so wound up I started with the pooper scooper story and by the time I got to the forbidden donuts the clerk and I were giddy. Turns out my bank forgot I called to say I was going to Florida, and they apologized for panicking about major fraud potential at a Dunkin' drive thru. I'm sure there is now a notation on my account that all my purchases should be viewed as suspicious.

While I was not suffering classic 'roid rage, it was surely a 'roid rush, with my mind spinning from column topics, to whether I needed a 2 a.m. peanut butter and jelly sandwich. Yes. Yes, I did.

Onward my brain hurried, as I inhaled both the PB&J and the latest news. A spurt of Trump's tweets had me verging on real 'roid rage, so I quickly turned to the *New York Times* crossword.

What's a five-letter word for 'rise?' S-T-A-N-D. Right! Could I? Yes! But I couldn't get down again. Time to take another muscle relaxer.

Midway through rapping the complete score of *Hamilton* I read the story about a moose that broke into a house in Wisconsin during a snowstorm and took refuge on the living room sofa. I looked at my own sofa, snuggled in, and came crashing down as the muscle relaxant outperformed the steroids and I fell into a long winter's nap. By morning, my back was still really, really sore but unspasmed. Relief washed over me.

"Want me to get you a Dunkin' Donuts coffee?" Bonnie asked.

"Yes, please. Better use cash."

I know shit will still happen. But from now on I'm asking somebody else to pick it up.

MAY 2019

Young, Scrappy, and Hungry

First off, that headline does not refer to me. Well, maybe the hungry part.

But on Thursday, April 18, just as the Mueller Report, about (*what I think are*) high crimes and misdemeanors was about to be published, Bonnie and I were not paying attention.

Barreling down the highway, with tickets for *Hamilton* that evening, we were cramming. I hadn't crammed like this since an all-nighter for my 1969 English Lit final.

But there we were, Bonnie driving, me reading aloud the rapping, rhyming, stunningly brilliant lyrics by Lin-Manuel Miranda, trying to catch and understand it all before curtain time. Yes, this is the first Broadway musical I've ever known to positively require homework.

Admittedly, the closest either of us had previously come to rap music was watching Ice-T on *Law and Order: SVU*. Some remedial rap education and hip-hop schooling was needed for these aficionados of Broadway shows like *Hello, Dolly!* and *Chicago*.

And, luckily, we were heading for the city of Chicago, where friends had procured the tickets for us. So we'd had six hours the day before, and six more hours on this day, to prep for our experience that evening.

As I finished reading the words for each number, we'd play it on the original cast recording and make sure we got not only the gist, but the nuance—and appreciate each internal rhyme, the genius concepts Miranda pulled from the biography of Alexander Hamilton, and the entire tale of the colonies rising up in revolution to defeat the British to free the thirteen colonies.

And just the way my caffeine-fueled, once-upon-a-time all-nighter ensured my success recalling Dickens, Thackeray, and the Brontë sisters, our cramming for *Hamilton* did the trick. We got it, we loved it; it may have been the most stunning, fully involving theater experience ever. How is it possible, after all the awards, all the press, all the publicity these past few years about *Hamilton*, that we did not find it over-hyped? It really is that good.

And bold, having us completely believe we were watching George Washington, Aaron Burr, and Thomas Jefferson, though these real-life figures of Western European ancestry were portrayed by actors of color. It was so exciting.

The staged story of how a bunch of "young, scrappy, and hungry" patriots, most under forty years of age, got the people in the colonies to start a revolution for their freedom resonates in 2019.

Don't tell me that at thirty-seven, Mayor Pete Buttigieg is too young to be president. He's older now than Hamilton, Jefferson, or Burr were when they incited a revolution and freed the colonies.

On stage, Alexander Hamilton talked, rapped, and sang about "Not throwing away my shot." I don't think that Pete Buttigieg, or any of the Democrats with their hats in the ring, should consider giving up their shot.

As Lin-Manuel Miranda wrote and the on-stage patriots sang:

> *Rise up ...*
> *Time to take a shot!*

Can a Broadway show incite another revolution? I hope so. For those of you who have seen the show, think about it.

And if you've not had the *Hamilton* experience, if you cannot get, afford, or conquer the logistics of getting a ticket, or even if you haven't the slightest interest in seeing this amazing show, I have some advice.

I suggest you get hold of the recording, grab a friend or two, have your favorite beverages and snacks on hand, and read and listen to the words. I bet you'll be surprised how much you love rapping along. And marveling at the sheer genius of the musical poetry of Lin-Manuel Miranda.

Then, rise up! Let's not throw away our shot. At the very least, not at the ballot box.

MAY 2019

The Human-Animal Bond: Stress? What Stress?

They say people with pets live longer.

Researchers at the American Veterinary Medical Association have found that the human-animal bond is a mutually beneficial and dynamic relationship, essential to the health and well-being of both species.

Well, yes, I may be 15 percent less likely to suffer heart trouble because of my bonding with my dog. But I'm 20 percent more likely to stroke out when startled awake by the unmistakable sound of a dog barfing.

They should market an alarm clock with a buzzer sounding like dog regurgitation. It's the only thing that gets me up like a shot.

It is, however, encouraging that these veterinary researchers attribute the following health benefits to our bonding with our companion animals.

Stress reduction: Hugging or petting a dog increases dopamine and serotonin in the brain to produce happiness. Wonderful.

But if petting my dog lowers my blood pressure, what does coming home to find only one shoe of each pair with a remaining insole do to it?

One of my previous schnauzers drooled and shook whenever I started cooking. It was surely caused by his PTSD over occasional smoke detector activation. But when guests asked, "Why is he drooling and shaking?" my answering "Because we're cooking," probably gave our guests stress.

My current schnauzer shrieks with a blood-curdling wail when I get out the Windex and paper towels to clean the tabletops. Between yelps, he bites at the spray bottle and remains hysterical the entire time. Both of our blood pressures rise.

Likewise, he attacks the vacuum cleaner like it's Freddy Krueger in a hockey mask. The Oreck has fang marks. What is it about our cooking and cleaning? My dogs, past and present, used our domestic activities to get everybody's blood pumping wildly through our arteries. To de-stress I'd have to hire a maid and a cook. *Ooooh,* good idea.

More physical activity: Sure, walking my dog gets me moving, but my prince, who hates the sun, is apt to sit down in the shade mid-walk and refuse to soldier on. My staggering home hefting twenty-five pounds of schnauzer is not the same as wearing one-pound ankle weights.

I think dramatic music activates his bladder. I get plenty of exercise jumping up to let him out, always at the most climactic moment of a TV show.

Likewise, he scratches at the door the second we sit down for dinner. I think this one is an attention grabber, but I don't want to be wrong. Not only don't I want the mess, but if I get out the paper towels and rug shampoo we start with the howling and blood pumping again.

Social connections: Pets allow numerous opportunities to interact and meet new people. Like at the dog beach. It's easy to make new friends when you have to grab your dog and say, "I'm so sorry he peed on your beach blanket."

Also, I meet people at the dog park because of my dog's aforementioned aversion to sunshine. He seeks out random strangers, sits in their shadow, and leans into the back of their legs so thoroughly some people fall over. "That's my dog; sorry, he loves that you were throwing shade."

Emotional support: Let's face it, this is the big one. Dogs are great at providing emotional support. Here he sits, right now, in his bed on the floor in my office as I type. He's always here for me.

And frankly, at this moment, I could use some emotional support.

"Windsor, help me. Can you think of any other weird things you do I can add to this article?"

I get nothing.

"C'mon, boy. I'm twenty minutes from deadline and I have writer's block. What other bonding things do you do that drive me batty?"

He gives me that pathetic head tilt.

My own head drops to the desk. I'm a hundred words short. Woe is me.

And there he is, paws on my legs, looking up at me, doing his best smiley face. I pick him up and he bestows kisses, wriggles in my arms, and gives me a big hug. And settles into my lap, Thanks, Windsor.

I've got 700 words and there's nothing like unconditional love.

MAY 2019

Damn Spam

Is your email inbox flooded with as much unwanted crap as mine?

I had to schedule an entire afternoon this week to unclog it. The very word *unsubscribe* now gives me the yips. And how did I get on these lists in the first place?

TeaParty.com? I saw it and wanted to drop my phone in Boston Harbor. I hit unsubscribe, and it told me it may take a short time to go into effect. November 2020? Egad, I hope not.

Then there was ScaliseforCongress. Seriously? That dude who had his life saved on the softball diamond by a brave lesbian police officer and he still votes anti-LGBTQ? I unsubscribed and it said, "sorry to see you go." Not as sorry as I was to see him recover having learned nothing.

I opted out of mail from the Center for Genetics and Society, and it gave me the option of checking "Oops, I made a mistake, re-subscribe me." Um, no mistake. I really don't want to read about test tube and designer babies.

Then there was the Puppies and Dog Lovers Group, offering to save homeless animals and give the first ten subscribers an iPhoneX. Puleeze. I know clickbait when I see it. But these creeps had the indecency to say "If you really hate puppies UNSUBSCRIBE here. Auuugggghhhh...

Wow. I hadn't seen this much spam since I collected canned goods to prepare for that phony Y2K scare at the turn of the millennium.

As for Schnauzer.com, trying to sell me schnauzer pajamas, sneakers, sheets, and earrings, I'm crying "Uncle!" Yes, they know a sucker for schnauzers when they see one, since I have already made a ridiculous purchase or two. But even I, resident at schnauzer Haven, have enough schnauzer T-shirts and hats. Scram!

And how do I stop daily emails from Evensi, inviting me to a tattoo parlor owner's birthday bash in Georgetown or the 10th Annual Taste of the Suburbs? What could that even be? Cheez Whiz canapes? Before Elvis left the building the site asked me if I was sure I wanted to give up hearing about 100 million events worldwide. Yes, yes, I do. My private jet is in the shop.

It's true, I did order a wad of business cards and a roll of stickers saying "Signed by the Author" from an online promotional company. Meanwhile, at the pace I sell books, the roll of stickers won't be depleted until 2037. But I get an email from the company six days a week. Hitting the ubiquitous unsubscribe got me a multiple choice: reduce special offers and big savings to once a week, hear about enormous discounts once a month, or unsubscribe completely and miss out. No FOMO—fear of missing out—here. Bye, Felicia.

I ask you, why would Samsonite try to sell me luggage once a week? It's a once a decade, if that, purchase. Ta-ta. But they wanted feedback about why I was unsubscribing. In the multiple choices there was no option for "because I am not Lady Gaga."

After three hours, I clicked unsubscribe on a site and was so grateful when it simply reported "You have been removed from the list," I wanted to re-up just to thank them.

And of course, there are the sites I appreciate but wear me out with daily pleas for donations. Yes, I back Protect Democracy, Joe Biden, and every other Democrat running for president, many other individual politicians, and a host of worthy causes. But enough already with the monsoon of Donate Now emails. Go away. Or I won't be able to afford Wi-Fi and none of your pleas will reach me.

As my frantic quest to clean out my inbox entered hour four and the clock ticked toward happy hour, I finally found a site encouraging me to express myself. "Tell us why you are unsubscribing from the Legislative Majority PAC."

I explained that I am inundated with email and though I support their cause, they should please forgive me for ditching their weekly missive. Instead of scrolling through pleas for cash I will spend my time and money for the next eighteen months standing on my head to support whichever candidate gets the nod to unseat our current president and doing my best to survive until November 2020.

That also means I'll be too busy to buy luggage, promotional stickers, or schnauzer-decorated socks. Although the socks tempt me.

I really wish I had the option of opting out of the deluge of unwanted email by forwarding every single subscription to Rep. Steve Scalise.

JUNE 2019

Hell No, We Won't Go!

Having just helped my stepmom move into a glorious but very expensive independent living senior apartment in Florida, I've been thinking a lot about where I'm going to continue aging gracelessly.

Luckily, I'm not in any hurry, since I learned, at my stepmom's new home orientation, that folks used to move to independent or assisted living facilities starting in their mid-seventies. Now it seems, it's happening much later, with people entering these residences in their late eighties. And at that, still enjoying Pilates classes, dances, and happy hour.

Wow, I hope this means I've got plenty of years before seeking communal help. In fact, while seventy may not be the optimistically new fifty, as has been touted, it does seem at least like the new sixty.

And, as baby boomers have always done, my generation continues to reinvent the culture. After all, we required the first split-session kindergartens, rioted on college campuses (I've inhaled my share of tear gas), and marched for and against all manner of things.

Picture me in a throng (no, not a thong) on the steps of the Lincoln Memorial, in my ratty bell bottoms, fringed vest, and ugly flower power necklace, chanting "Hell No, We Won't Go!" with my draft-age boyfriends. That's why it now seems natural to me to be hollering "Hell No, We Won't Go" to the nursing home.

Boomers are finding creative, lower cost substitutes for 401(k)-sucking senior living. I just read in *USA Today* about a guy who intends to spend his golden years going from hotel chain to hotel chain in famous resort towns, saving money and getting great service. Not to mention free shampoo.

Why would I need to leave home? Down the road I can use my AARP discount for an inexpensive hotel room (especially off-season) with a free hot breakfast, complimentary soap, and the luxury of staying in my favorite resort. If a medium-cost independent living home averages $150 to $200 a day, I can stay out on Route One for a lot less than that! At some places I can even get a gym, pool, and a free cookie in the lobby at 4 p.m.

If, by chance, I win the lottery I can join the adventurous seniors now eschewing ultra high-end senior facilities for the ultra-high seas. As it turns out, it costs less to live year-round on a fancy cruise ship than in a fancy independent living facility. I'd get three meals a day, an onboard doctor, laundry, and maid service plus Broadway entertainers and a casino. Not to mention the Strait of Gibraltar, South of France, or Carnival in Rio.

Snopes says this is happening although the cost differential has narrowed. If I stayed on board long enough, in addition to world travel I suppose I would eventually get a cheap burial at sea. Oh, and until the end, I wouldn't have to drive at night anymore.

But if there's anything to make me want to spend my golden years at home on the Delaware Coast, it's a glimpse of what Rehoboth Beach aging in place could be, based on an incident I was involved in last week.

Driving to happy hour, we took a turn a bit short, and our passenger side rear tire hit the curb with a loud scrape.

We appeared to still be on a roll, so we continued on and parked in front of a neighborhood gay bar. After dinner, drinks, drag queens etc., we came out to discover we had a painfully flat tire.

As we looked up the number for Triple A, a young woman came flying out of the restaurant shouting, "Ma'am, Ma'am, I can help you!" Whereupon she popped the trunk, grabbed the tire wrench, and attacked the task with bravado and gusto. She even jumped up and down on the lug nut wrench to loosen the hardware – a fun show winning the admiration of the growing crowd.

"This is what baby dykes are for!" she hollered, proudly finishing up the job.

Feeling like elders, we thanked her profusely, offered a tip that was refused, and finally, many a thank-you later, went on our merry way.

"You know, I said to Bonnie, "Aging in place might not be so bad. Once we get used to being called ma'am and letting the youngsters help, this could be fun."

Our imaginations went wild, picturing a system of meals on wheels from our favorite gay bars, hiring good-looking baby dykes to run errands for us, and even hiring live-in help uniformed in rainbow T-shirts and sensible shoes.

You know, I think I'll love spending my (hopefully) still far-off golden years at our resort of last resort. I'm hoping to be in my 90s, hunkered down at home or in a lovely motel along Route One, up to my ears in free shampoo and complimentary 4 p.m. cookies. And baby dykes. Lots of them.

Who's in?

JUNE 2019

What Do You Meme I'm Old?

If you're a Luddite like me, do you know what a meme is? I needed it explained to me long after I should have known what it was, so I suspect there are folks reading this who have no idea.

According to Facebook, a meme is an idea, behavior, or style that spreads, person to person, within a culture—like gifs (moving memes), jokes, or continuing transmissions over the internet of a certain theme. On Facebook, one of my favorites was the photo of former President Obama with his VP Joe Biden, laughing. People online invented hundreds of captions for it, and a meme was born.

These days, there's a really fun meme going around in answer to the question "How old are you?"

The response might be "I'm a pack of Camels for 35 cents old," or "I'm the flashbulb didn't go off old," or my recent favorite, "I'm tin foil on the TV antenna old."

I'm Encyclopedia Britannica with a payment plan old.

I'm party-line phone old.

I'm getting a color TV old.

I'm *Gilligan's Island* in prime time old.

And I'm Annette Funicello and Mickey Mouse Club old.

And just as I was smiling at this online nostalgia meme, I got a CNN alert on my phone that our White House emperor without clothes had just come out against the Equality Act, which, in a historic first, passed in the House of Representatives.

It's the legislation banning discrimination against LGBTQs based purely on who we are. Such a simple idea. Protect us from discrimination in employment, housing, public accommodations, education, federal funding, and the jury system. Actual equality.

But alas, it will almost certainly not pass in the Senate.

And while it's by no means a surprise that the grand poohbah is against equality for us, it's increasingly scary. I remember the bad old days our government wants to bring back.

I'm you could go to jail for just being gay old.

I'm don't dare come out at the office old.

I'm you could get killed for holding hands in public old.

I'm gay bars only in bad neighborhoods old.

In fact, I became legal drinking age on June 29, 1969, only twenty-four hours after the first bottle was thrown at the Stonewall Inn riots, a half century ago. While the four nights of rioting continued downtown in Greenwich Village, I spent that birthday uptown, reading in the *New York Times* about Judy Garland's funeral the day before and then going to see a Broadway show that night. I also remember seeing a tiny, snarky article in the *New York Daily News* about homosexuals rioting in the Village. The headline was "Homo Nest Raided—Queen Bees Stinging Mad." I honestly don't remember what I thought of that homophobic blather.

I did not yet understand or admit to myself I was a homosexual or know I would someday claim that riot and rebellion downtown as part of my history.

Which is why my friend Mike Gilles and I recently put together a show called *Voices from Stonewall*. We felt the need to celebrate those brave gay kids, trans women, drag queens, and butch lesbians, diverse in color and gender expression, who had the guts to fight back that night. They fueled the revolution that was already brewing in Philadelphia, San Francisco, New York, and Washington, DC.

And as we celebrate them, we are being reminded daily about the fragile nature of our advances and how easily our rights, including marriage equality, can be taken away again. The phrase "settled law" does not seem to resonate with the current Supreme Court.

I want to absorb the feisty courage and determination of the

Stonewall class of '69 and let their words and actions energize me.

Yes, I'm Stonewall old.

I'm March on Washington '78, '87, '93, 2000 old.

Our show was performed at CAMP Rehoboth on June 22, part of our Pride celebrations. It felt wonderful and necessary to celebrate our pioneers.

And, depending on what happens next, I can honestly say: I'm take to the streets old, but not so old I won't do it again.

JUNE 2019

The Kids are All Right

This Pride Month, with a mash-up of joyous rainbow events and discouraging anti-gay controversy, I absorbed the news with a yo-yo of emotions.

Rainbow flags and celebrations are everywhere. But what about the rainbow crosswalks defaced in several cities? The blowback from various city pride proclamations?

Florida's Gov. DeSantis removed all LGBTQ references from the Pulse Nightclub anniversary proclamation. It's like nobody died and they're commemorating the loss of a concrete building. Oh dear, they lost how many windows and toilets? Thoughts and prayers for the toilets.

And then, our emperor with ill-fitting white tie and tails ordered US embassies overseas NOT to fly the rainbow flag for Pride month. How cruel and insulting is that? Many embassy staffs stuck their collective necks out, defied orders, risked their diplomatic careers, and flew the flag anyway. Bravo for them! Shame on our faithless leader.

There was a Catholic bishop who urged his flock not to attend any pride parades, and worse, a minister who called, from the pulpit, for the death of homosexuals. Yes, his superiors silenced him, but they let him retire with full respect. Yuck.

Then, omigod, a trio of straight guys applied to the City of Boston for a permit for a so-called Straight Pride March. Did they even need a permit? Isn't every day straight pride day? And imagine a pride parade without glitter, Gloria Gaynor, and feathers. Coors and khaki pants are not that interesting. Who's the grand marshal, Judge Kavanaugh?

Twitter exploded. "The Heteros are Upseteros!," "A straight parade can be seen daily in the checkout line at Cosco," and

"Mandatory socks and sandals!"

So what's the meaning of all this? Some folks feel these bigoted activities and high-profile Nazi-like (or in some cases, actual Nazi) actions are a sign our community is going backwards on the journey toward equality.

I disagree and hope I'm right.

I suspect it's all a sign that we're winning. Our hard-won marriage equality and widening mainstream acceptance has really pissed off the continuously shrinking cesspool of anti-gay haters.

With every rainbow flag they see, all the rainbow bunting on government or corporate property, every TV ad with same-sex couples, every Stonewall documentary on CNN, every Pride celebration, they're panicking and peeing themselves in fear. They're showing off their prejudice, trying to act powerful, but they're cowering in their camouflage T-shirts. They're the real sissies.

It strengthened my position when I read about the 100 people, two from each state, honored by the *Advocate Magazine* as their 2019 Champions of Pride.

Steve Newman, president of Delaware Pride, was a Champion, and full disclosure here, I was the second Delawarean tapped. While I'm overwhelmed by the honor, I also noted I'm the oldest person on the list. As Mother Burnside bellows in the musical *Mame*, "Pass me my shawl and cane, I feel the winds of change!"

And positive change is coming. Learning about the accomplishments and agendas of all these young champions, from all over the country, gives me such hope. Even the new terminology they use to identify themselves is exciting. There are plenty of gays, lesbians, and queers noted, but also these self-identified champions: lumberjack lesbian, demi-sexual, nonbinary queer, gender fluid, trans-masculine-queer-identified, bisexual-disabled two spirit, nonbinary androgynous, and more.

If this stodgy old editor can violate the rules of grammar 101 and use the plural word "they" to describe a singular person, we all can.

And from what I hear, the plural and singular "theys" are all working like crazy to advance LGBTQ+ (that "+" would be all those new names!) equality. And they are also pooling their talents with their straight political allies to form effective campaigns for victories in the 2020 elections.

Two days after this edition of *Letters* hits the streets and screens, this plain old vanilla lesbian will take the bus from Rehoboth to Greenwich Village for the Pride parade celebrating the 50th Anniversary of the Stonewall riots. I cannot wait.

And later in the week, I intend to celebrate Independence Day with pride in my country that I may have lacked since November 2016. I'll celebrate knowing that like-minded patriots are already kicking ass, getting folks registered to vote, stirring up enthusiasm, and working to wrest control of our country from the self-interested haters and dangerous demagogues.

When those July Fourth fireworks go off, let's launch a busy fifteen months of political patriotism to save our nation.

I'm all in. Me, Thee, and They.

JULY 2019

A Weekend of Firsts

For a weekend it was quite spectacular. For a birthday weekend—not even a BIG important birthday, it was possibly the best ever. All accompanied by a series of firsts.

On Saturday, June 29, my actual birthday, I walked outside to discover that my first-ever personally owned tomato plant had a round green orb growing on it. For a gal who grew up thinking tomatoes were birthed in a container, enclosed in cellophane, this was a revelation. I will keep you posted.

After a marvelous meal prepared by our bestie boyfriends, we hit several ocean block and boardwalk watering holes, followed by a quick visit to the Funland horse races. Ever played? You roll Skee-balls into various point-accumulating holes, and the more points you accrue the faster your metal horse trots across the silly scoreboard. I've been trying to win a race for the last twenty-six years. Nada. On Saturday night my horse won by a nose, bells rang, and nobody revealed how much my pals paid the carny worker to have me win.

At dawn the next morning when I saw a dozen Subaru Outbacks parked at Lowe's, I knew there was a CAMP Rehoboth bus trip departing. Another first—I was awake before Dunkin' Donuts opened.

As the bus roared toward the Big Apple, I got a text from Speaker of the House Pete Schwartzkopf. It said "Whoa, front page above the fold!" Yup, I looked and there I was, with five other Delawareans of a certain age, on the front page of the *News Journal*, talking about our memories of 1969 and the meaning of the Stonewall anniversary. Cool. Or it would have been if it hadn't been the shittiest photo of me ever taken. Oy, a first and a worst.

So, we got to midtown Manhattan by 11 a.m. for World Pride Day and the fiftieth Anniversary of Stonewall. Yes, there really were four million people in the streets surrounding the miles-long parade route.

On our way to Fiftth Avenue for the official parade, we crossed paths with a protest parade, with marchers celebrating the lives of Stonewall heroes and very serious gay rights and human rights causes. They marched separately to decry the creeping commercialism of the official parade. We cheered for these earnest marchers and soldiered on.

After being sucked into a swell of humanity moving like volcanic lava across Twenty-Third street to the parade, I am thrilled to report I was not trampled to death. But neither was I able to get closer to the street than a wall of people ten-deep in front of me. Consequently, all I saw of the parade were high-flying balloons, queens on stilts, tops of high hair, waving flags, and a few two-story floats. I stood amid cheering, screaming, happy people and heard the Dykes on Bikes loud and clear.

I got a pretty good contact high, got glitter-bombed, met the most amazing youngsters, saw an extraordinary number of overflowing bosoms escaping flimsy clothing, delighted in clever signs, all manner of rainbow T-shirts, lots of celebrating allies, young butches, old butches, gym bunnies, leather guys, fathers with strollers, drag queens and kings, senior citizens, and all—and I mean ALL—manner of queer life.

We also fortified ourselves, retreating to boisterous rainbow-adorned bars where, by the way, everyone, binary, nonbinary, gay, straight, bi, or trans, hollered "Happy Pride." I think the straight bartenders had more fun than usual.

In a stunning first, we stood for forrty-five minutes at a McDonald's in a line of people waiting to pee. I know, it sounds terrible. But it was joyous, astonishing, invigorating, and finally, a great relief.

So, here's my takeaway. 1969 was amazing. I was twenty-one. Stonewall, Woodstock, Man on the Moon, you name it. I'm glad I was there then to experience it all and here now to experience the half century of aftershocks.

For some celebrants, especially the youngsters, this was a glorious and giddy joyful event. For many, like me, it was millions of people, their governments, big corporations, foreign visitors, and much more, repudiating the idea of the closet for queers. It was one humongous International Coming Out Day and I felt liberated as never before.

There will be glitter in the New York City streets until 2034.

As for the celebration itself, I do think gay life was much, much harder in the old days, when we were outlaws, but getting up front to watch a pride parade back then was much, much easier. I walked 14,000 steps before the battery died on my phone and who knows how many more dragging my sorry ass back to the bus.

It was epic to be among the mega-millions celebrating being out and proud in 2019. I'm queer and I'm still here. Imagine that.

JULY 2019

Don't Cry for Me, Marie Kondo; the Truth Is I Never Got You...

I finally relaxed when I found out that the Marie Kondo method of decluttering is wrong for me,

You know Marie, the Japanese guru of tidying up and tossing out anything that doesn't spark joy. I took to her right away, throwing out my vacuum cleaner and Crock-Pot. The last sparks I got from those devices were from frayed cords.

But Marie is relentless, selling millions of copies of her books on KonMari, organizing, and giving collectors like me, just one souvenir short of an appearance on *Hoarders*, a guilt complex.

Frankly, most of my home is in pretty good shape. We downsized and now have a lovely great room where we can age in place in our new matching recliners. We jettisoned lots of stuff before the move, sending the china service for twelve to the thrift store and the sterling silver, which apparently nobody wants anymore, to be melted down in exchange for a trip to Paris. Don't judge me.

But my tiny office in the trailer, I mean manufactured home, is the problem. Kondo talks about getting your life back by purging your stuff. I don't need to get my life back. I still have it; the evidence clogs all eight-by-eight feet of my cubbyhole office.

But Marie made me ashamed and feel like a clutterbug with my crammed bookshelves, bulging file cabinets, and framed photo collages threatening to pull down the flimsy walls—not to ignore the sentimental doodads and geegaws on just about every inch of every single surface.

I began to purge files but wound up in a nostalgia parade, down the rabbit hole of prom pictures, a 1983 Back Porch

Restaurant menu, copies of my first articles from *Delaware Beach Life*, and a twenty-four-year-old photo of me, thirty-five pounds lighter, with natural brown hair, standing in front of Dolle's on the boardwalk. If I stood there now, I'd cover up the entire word Popcorn, not just the Pop part.

Then there's my other affliction, also from the Japanese. Apparently, I am a proponent of Tsundoku: the practice of buying more books than you can ever read, piling up tomes for some future date without deadlines and editing chores. If Suduko is for numbers, Tsundoku is for all the words I mean to read but don't.

Face it, I flunked KonMari 101.

Then the strangest thing happened. I went to a writer's conference where one of my heroes, Dorothy Allison, author of the mega-award-winning *Bastard Out of Carolina* gave a masterclass on getting our writer's juices flowing; plumbing our past for memoir; and using the beloved detritus from a life well-lived to inspire us.

"I have an altar," she loudly proclaimed, not in a house of worship, but in her office. That altar is her bookshelf, crammed with already-read and yet-to-be-devoured books. Then, the writer described the six inches of shelf space in front of all her books, where she keeps her special souvenirs of a literary and personal life well-lived—her awards, souvenirs, framed snapshots, collected shells, and other meaningful dust-collectors that inspire her imagination, memories, and writing life.

Well, my book-stuffed shelves are narrower, with only four inches for my altar. But there are my icons: a miniature painted dolphin from the 2002 Rehoboth Dolphin Project; a tiny, plastic, head-bobbing moose from Nova Scotia; bone-shaped tags from schnauzers gone but not forgotten; several small wooden storefront blocks bought at Browseabout Books, depicting favorite Rehoboth watering holes; a clear glass square with an imprinted CAMP Rehoboth logo commemorating my nineteen years on their Board; a matchbox car painted like a New York City yellow cab; and on and on.

I love my totems, my talismans, my books waiting to be read—or not. I sit surrounded by this altar, writing this piece, inspired.

Sorry, Marie Kondo, the only book I managed to part with was yours.

JULY 2019

I Have Reservations

Let me talk to you about my lifestyle. And no, not the way that term is hurled by anti-gay haters.

Yes, I'm talking about an L-word, but it's not lesbian. It's more likely lunch. And dinner. It's about my lifestyle of dining out. I do it a lot and always have.

But last week, Bonnie and I realized we'd eaten wonderful meals, at home, for six nights out of the past seven. Okay, friends, I see you gasping and clutching your pearls.

I didn't even have that many dinners at home in a row when I was eight years old.

Seriously, I didn't grow up at the dining room table. I can count on two hands and a foot how many times I sat with my sister and parents having a meal in our own home.

My childhood was great. Dinner at home, not so much. My wonderful mother was a horrible cook, with neither interest nor talent. My beloved Jewish grandmother tried to pass along chopped liver and blintz recipes, but nothing took.

In my house, incinerated flounder squares meant fish, vegetables arrived gray from eternity on the stove, and chicken came from a precooked rotisserie spit at the grocery.

Through junior high I lived in the suburbs, and my Madison Avenue mad-man dad wouldn't get home from Manhattan until 7 p.m. We kids gobbled spaghetti or burgers at 5:30 and the parents had the second seating—often going out and leaving us with a sitter.

On weekends, we all dined out. At a seafood house on Long Island Sound, I savored what fish was supposed to taste like. I learned of French bistro food, sampled German spaetzle and Italian eggplant Parmesan, and pretty much aced my homeschooled food appreciation course.

I loved *Ozzie and Harriet* dinners at my friends' houses, but I loved my wacky family dining dynamics too.

By high school, we'd moved to Manhattan. My father's career dictated frequent business dinners and socializing. And when there were no obligations, my parents had the whole exciting Big Apple restaurant scene to conquer. Lots of times they took us along to Chinatown, Little Italy, or hole-in-the-wall eateries.

When my sister and I were left on our own, there was a house account at the Stage Deli, two blocks from the apartment. Maybe three nights a week we'd go for baked chicken, corned beef brisket, or matzo ball soup. The huge menu gave us diverse choices and we'd just sign for it. I also got to sit next to celebrities, like Walter Cronkite, the Smothers Brothers, and Carol Burnett. Good times.

Through high school and then college vacations, while my parents played, my friends and I ate Nathan's hot dogs, New York slices of pizza, or the fare at a zillion neighborhood diners.

During my pre-Rehoboth career years, my newspaper job as theater and restaurant critic didn't help, but it sure was fun. In 1982 Bonnie joined up, and we were out many weeknights reviewing or grabbing a quick bite before evening rehearsals for my theater jobs.

Dining out is in my DNA. It feeds my soul as well as my stomach. It's nature *and* nurture. I am what I am. Baby I was born this way. Even as I've tried over the years, for both dietary and financial reasons, to change the dynamic and dine home more, I've had poor to middling results.

Enter retirement. Ish. Clearly, I'm still working a little, but a mostly fixed income dictates lifestyle choices. So, after decades of eating out, we've vowed to get to know our own kitchen a little more.

And it's working out really well. First, Bonnie has become

an excellent cook and a killer griller. I shop, she cooks, I do dishes. We try to eat healthy, but keep Nathan's hot dogs and grandma's matzo balls in the mix. Home on the range, we allow no gray mushy veggies or cremated fish.

Having friends join us around the table is wonderful too, adding that little social buzz and social pulse I crave.

We joined Costco, but in keeping the freezer full, we learned not to over-buy. Just say "no" to a matched set of humongous jelly jars lasting two people well into the next millennium. We roll through the store muttering "nothing we don't really need." An occasional bag of Snickers sneaks through.

And we try to keep Windsor from freaking out when the crispy chicken wing tips occasionally set off the smoke detector.

Will I disappear from local restaurants and bar stools? No way. My inherited restaurant hopping spirit rages on. I'm just adding a little balance.

I'll be having my cake and eating it too. At home.

AUGUST 2019

No Place Like It

I was tasked with writing an article for the annual real estate issue of a magazine and it got me thinking about settlements and stuff.

As I age gracelessly, I've had, gulp, seven decades of experience with real estate. I came from a New York City apartment and moved to a variety of city and suburban townhouses and homes. Over my quarter of a century on the Delaware Coast I have lived in almost every type of shelter known to mortgage companies.

I started out on a boat in a slip on Rehoboth Bay. It was so long ago we ran an actual landline phone down the dock. We were young, we didn't wear enough SPF sunscreen, and it was fun for weekends while we worked and had a real house near Baltimore.

That first summer, we purchased a three-bedroom condo in town, steps to the boardwalk. We rented it out in the "season" while we stayed on the boat. Thanks to the 1995 real estate recession, we bought the place for a song ("Those were the days my friend") and we could cover our entire condo mortgage and expenses with rental income. Now the song is Brenda Lee's "I'm sorry, so sorry."

My landlord adventures were 90 percent great, 10 percent having to dig pretzels out of my VHS recorder, and replace carpet eaten by a colossal English mastiff.

In 1998, tired of mildew, we sold the boat and bought a second Rehoboth condo. It was a tiny studio with a Murphy bed, so we had a bedroom and living room, but not at the same time. We also had dedicated parking in the midst of town. I called the condo my $74,000 parking space and it was worth every penny. We loved summer weekends there, and the rest of the year at the more substantial condo near the boardwalk.

By the turn of the millennium, we'd giddily doubled our money on both dwellings and sold them. Schmucks!!! If we'd held on, I'd be writing this column from my house in Tuscany. But no, we thought we were real estate geniuses and cashed in to buy a single-family house two miles from the beach.

Living near the ocean full time by then, our new home had an enormous yard, spacious rooms, a giant kitchen (odd, as we mostly made reservations), and all the life-sucking expenses that went with it. At closing it was the little house on the prairie, so we spent thousands of dollars buying, planting, and nurturing more than thirty Leyland Cypress trees.

And yes, we thought we'd rent our full-time home out for a month in the "season," too, taking refuge in our other mortgaged asset, a twenty-eight-foot recreational vehicle.

You've not lived until you've played *Survivor* for a month, baking in the August sun, ensconced in an aluminum tube at an RV park out of town. The summer rental was one and done. But we did spend fourteen great years in that house. We knew it was time to downsize when the same trees that cost us thousands of dollars to plant now cost thousands of dollars to be "topped" and pruned by people in bucket trucks.

Where to next? We wanted the privacy of a single-family home, but without the maintenance. So we sold our house and settled on a manufactured home on rented land. I call it the Greenwich Connecticut of trailer parks.

For once, I think we made a smart move. Although my long-suffering Realtor, who had been through it all with us, kept cautioning "Are you sure you can live in this?" He knew our penchant for architectural columns, tray ceilings and crown molding. Besides, the place desperately needed a complete overhaul and a full face-lift.

I have to say, it was a delight when he attended our housewarming and exclaimed "It's an effing miracle."

Listen, the manufactured home cost a fraction of what we made selling our house. And the annual land rent is pretty much equal to what we'd previously paid for mowing, mulching, irrigating, tree-pruning, driveway black-topping, snow removal, and interest on our Lowes credit card.

Now, our annual tax bill is lower than dinner for two; my deed is registered at the DMV (honest); there are gorgeous cherry trees and well-tended flower beds; and we don't have to mow it, mulch it, or feed it. We have a community pool and exercise room, and finally, we can lock the door and travel with the money we didn't spend lopping tops off trees.

So, by this time we have lived in every kind of real estate there is but a yurt. Stay tuned. It could happen.

SEPTEMBER 2019

Days of Wine and Roses

This was supposed to be a fun column for the Labor Day edition, the deadline to occur during my ten-day vacation.

Not knowing if I'd have Wi-Fi aboard ship, I left behind a perfectly adequate column about the joys of dining with dogs on Rehoboth restaurant patios.

A writer plans and the Delaware Division of Public Health laughs.

While I was trotting around France, a little-known state regulation banning dogs on restaurant patios reared its head. Seriously? And I'm about to publish a puff piece hawking the joys of brunching in public with our best friends?

Hold the presses. I texted home to pull the column, and instead I am in Normandy, France, thumbing a replacement column on my phone.

We've sailed the Seine from Paris to the beaches of Normandy, seeing Van Gogh's wheat fields and Monet's water lilies. In Rouen we photographed sixteenth-century buildings and sampled the apple "cider" of the region.

It's an Olivia Riverboat cruise, so my wife and I have been with 125 other lesbians, enjoying a fabulous week of wine, women, and song. And croissants. Escargot. Champagne.

Comic musician Lisa Koch is onboard. She spontaneously came up with a song about the lone female crew member athletically handling the lines on the ship's bow as a hundred queer girls ogled her from the cocktail lounge. I'm sure Lisa has apologies for Sondheim for the new lyrics to "Maria," which had us, including crew member Maria, howling with laughter.

As we drove by bus to one of the picturesque towns, our local guide told us all about the history of the area and pointed out marvelous sights—including the church where she was recently married. Then she added "to a woman!" And the passengers erupted in congratulatory cheers.

We saluted Joan of Arc, rode a tethered hot air balloon over Paris, met some delightful women from all over the country, and made sure to take a photo with the six Rehoboth gals aboard—each of us holding a copy of *Letters*.

Today, we lunched at a French farmhouse liberated in 1944, and wound up at Omaha Beach and the American cemetery there, still decorated for last June's seventy-fifth anniversary of D-Day.

There are over 9,000 U.S soldiers buried there. We placed roses on the monuments.

I gazed out on the beach where so many Americans fell or risked their lives, and tears rolled down my face—not just for those brave soldiers, but for my country, which in many ways is behaving increasingly as our sworn enemies did in the 1940s.

What have we become? How do we fight for our democracy? How do we quell the hate and reclaim our national reputation for having room for all?

As I write this, we've got two more days of strong coffee, baguettes, art, sightseeing, and fine red wines. My veins are full of pure lard by now.

But when we get home, first, I'm hoping the canine patio issue gets resolved so I can run my column celebrating (a dietetic) brunch with Fido.

But more importantly, I hope the lesson I took from the D-Day landing sites propels me to work like crazy to fight and help win the 2020 battle of the ballot box. I hope you'll join me. For the memory of those more than 9,000 Americans buried in Normandy and many more all over the world, we can do nothing less.

SEPTEMBER 2019

One of These Days, Alice, Right to the Moon

What is it with the heavens these days? We're preoccupied with looking up.

Remember when there was one moon in the news? It came in white with small, medium, large, and plus size. It reportedly was made of green cheese, occasionally looked like a crescent roll, and had a cow jumping over it. Ralph Kramden, in early TV's *The Honeymooners*, constantly threatened to send his wife Alice there.

Now, it's not so simple. There are supermoons, micromoons, wolf moons, and worm moons, all discussed incessantly by Neil deGrasse Tyson. The worm moon happens in spring, ostensibly when the early bird gets the worm. The Dakota Sioux called it Moon When Eyes are Sore from Bright Snow. My spouse's hillbilly ancestors called it Moon When Eyes are Sore from Moonshine. Possibly followed by Gasping Moon from outrunning revenue men.

But yes, a Blue Moon has been around for a while, mostly in popular music and beer. But now when we talk about a Blue Moon it's all about science and astronomy. with news that industrial smoke and dust particles cause the moon to look hazy and blueish.

Sometimes, a Blue Moon is a second full moon within a given period, but that's hard to notice since everyone's fixating on the moon's new color palette. It's like a flip chart from Sherwin Williams.

When the full moon rose last April, it was called a Pink Moon, but it wasn't the slightest bit pink. According to the *Farmer's Almanac* the name heralded the appearance of the tiny pink petals on the phlox plant. It was also called the Egg Moon.

Heralding Humpty Dumpty?

The orange moon happens when there's a scattering of light around the horizon, which is a nice way of saying it's caused entirely by diesel exhaust, smoke fumes, and other disgusting air pollution.

But wait! Our September moon is called the Full Harvest Moon, set to appear on September 14, to herald the September 22 Autumnal Equinox. According to those chatty farmers, it provides the most light when you need it, for harvesting crops or salt water taffy on the still-busy boardwalk.

As obsessed with outer space as we've become, what's with Mars? Is there water ice on Mars or not? And is it real Philly Italian Ice in raspberry or lemon? Hey, if there's ice, it's so exciting, as it would enable cocktails and thus sustain life.

Last June, according to NASA, the Mars Explorer vehicle Curiosity discovered a huge plume of methane gas on the planet. Are Martians into food truck tacos?

I just read that NASA teams are exploring both Mars and its two moons, Phobos and Deimos, which sounds like an accounting firm. So now we have those two new moons to moon about along with our other heavenly obsessions. One of my obsessions is Moon Pie from Rehoboth's Blue Moon restaurant but I'm off topic here.

It seems even our current president is obsessed with the wild blue yonder. In his July Fourth message he announced, "We're going back to the moon soon and planting the American flag on Mars."

It's only fair that he should be the first to go.

Meanwhile, I'm still pissed off about Pluto. Ever since its 1930 discovery, this tiny orb has been a full-fledged planet. Until, in 2006, some rogue astronomers decided it was several asteroids shy of a clean plate and demoted it to a dwarf planet. Yes, you cannot be a planet unless you have removed debris and small objects around your orbit. Seriously. Give that planet a leaf blower and give it back its status.

So here we are, looking to the heavens for answers to life's mysteries. Personally, I think we should focus back on Earth and solve our own mysteries—like what exactly are Pop-Tarts? Are American Ninja Warrior athletes even human? Is there more than a two-minute off-season in Coastal Delaware?

And most importantly, I want to shout, 'One of these days, POTUS, straight to the moon!"

OCTOBER 2019

You Gotta Have Heart . . .

I'm stressing out.

Seriously. I'm in the doctor's office waiting for a cardiac stress test. Fortunately, I'm symptom free, and it's just a baseline test. But the nurse just shot some kind of liquid into my veins to make my heart race, causing me to stress.

Like I'm not already stressed over Trumpty Dumbty, a fluctuating 401(k), RBG's health, Amazonian fires, and Costco.

Don't get me wrong, I love Costco. But last week we used a tank of gas to get there and back to save five dollars on toilet paper. Rationalizing this is stressful.

At Costco we try to ignore anything we can't use up before going into assisted living. Following our last binge, come the apocalypse, all that will remain will be cockroaches, Cher, and our second humongous jar of Skippy peanut butter.

Having loaded our glut of goodies into the car, we head to WaWa to spend six dollars on ice cubes to protect the lamb chops we got for six dollars off.

Back home, the real stress hits. We cram the fridge and freezer to bursting but run out of closet and cabinet space to stash the mammoth cases of toilet paper, plastic bags, dinner napkins, and laundry supplies.

"Hey, let's buy a cabinet for behind the sofa to store all this stuff," I suggest, knowing full well we are now completely bonkers.

After searching Wayfair and Overstock.com, we realize just how stupid this is, but instead of giving up we go furniture shopping to eye $800 breakfronts. Finally, we hit the Habitat for Humanity thrift store.

Hallelujah! We find a good-looking credenza, creepily

matching our living room furniture, for just $125 plus delivery.

So, I'm in the doctor's waiting room, heart racing from injected chemicals, musing over this insanity, knowing I'm prepping for the stress test by stressing overspending money on gas, ice, and furniture for crap's sake, so I can save twelve bucks.

"Ms. Jacobs, we're almost ready for you."

So is the straitjacket.

"Please drink two cups of water from this cooler before we hook you up to the electrodes."

I obey. Naturally, by the time I'm flat on my back with the MRI thingy over my head, I have to pee. *Added stress.*

Then the technician says, "Place your left arm over your head, stay still and try not to take deep breaths." I had no intention of breathing deeply before she said that, but now, I'm desperate to do so. So, it's fifteen minutes of struggling not to suck air or scratch my suddenly itchy nose. *Stress much?*

I finish the test, take a delicious deep breath, and return to the waiting room to pause forty-five minutes until the resting heart rate test. Luckily the TV is not on Fox News.

I check my phone. I can read all Facebook posts just fine, but the app will not allow me to comment on anything. Seriously? That's like fitting me with a muzzle. *Resting heart rate, ha!*

I poke at the app, furiously trying and failing to add comments. *Mega-stress.* My only hope is to delete the entire app and reinstall it.

My phone asks "Are you sure you want to delete Facebook and all its contents?"

No! I'm not sure! But I plunge, deleting the entire Facebook app. I immediately reinstall the app, but before I can check if I'm back online or have just deleted a dozen years of my life, I hear "Ms. Jacobs, we are ready for you now." *What resting heart rate?* I've morphed from simple stress to full-on panic.

Apparently, I survived the test. And while the full results won't be available for another week, I probably didn't flunk, as they did not instantly rush me to the ER.

Later, back in the car, I check Facebook and I'm still alive online as well. *Whew.*

Heart rate resting, I head home, knowing we've got plenty of baggies and aluminum foil to last past the 2020 election. And I won't have to navigate around towering packs of toilet paper like in a hoarder house.

So what if we paid through the nose to house cheap Kleenex? So what if I miss a Facebook posting? Who cares if the E-ZPass tolls were more than I saved on chicken wings? Don't sweat the small stuff, Jacobs.

As for the big stuff, it's good to know my heart is pumping like it should. Let's just hope Justice Ginsburg's keeps doing the same.

NOVEMBER 2019

Wazy Lazy Days

Be afraid, be very afraid. Especially when you're driving with the Waze app in your car.

Waze is the latest, and some say greatest, GPS app on your phone. It supplies driving directions and finds alternate routes with real-time traffic info. Waze calculates shorter routes when it's going to be a long waze to Tipperary.

The app is Triple A TripTik meets crowd sourcing. Everybody on the road has an opinion, and they report it all to Waze. And I do like it, but in some waze it makes me crazy.

It's a fearmonger. There's an on-screen button to report an upcoming hazard. See something, say something. Okay, good to know. But when that artificially intelligent voice reports "Hazard ahead!" I panic, looking for a dead body in the road. Or a pallet of two-by-fours plopped in the left lane. But no, it's just a car on the shoulder.

So, I keep calm and carry on.

"Hazard ahead!"

Now I'm on full alert, but nothing happens. A quarter mile up, there's an '83 Buick off to the side with a belching radiator. This is not a hazard. It's antique roadshow.

Every day, at least ten times, Waze screams "Hazard ahead!" and it's always disappointing. Liar, liar, radiator on fire.

"Hazard ahead!"

I do not consider a Jeep on the shoulder with four guys in paintball outfits running to pee in the woods a hazard for anybody but unsuspecting squirrels.

"Hazard ahead!"

By this time, I'm starting to hallucinate, picturing King Kong in the center lane or Daisy Duke of Hazzard in her orange

Dodge Charger spun across the roadway. Geez, I notice my left blinker is accidentally flashing, and I start to wonder if I'm the hazard ahead.

Then comes "Police reported ahead!"

You know immediately which cars use Waze because we all slam on our brakes. This is a terrible hazard for people *not* using this app as they're likely to plow into the rest of us.

My least favorite Waze feature is the map that pops up telling me how many drivers around me are using Waze. It's hundreds of them.

But why do I care? Is this a dating app? Do they want me to flag down another user and arrange a date at the Smyrna Rest Stop?

Also, there are alerts from advertisers, so your Waze announces a nearby MacDonald's or Chick-fil-A.

Okay, I will admit I sometimes stop at Chick-fil-A ... don't judge ...

I have NEVER, EVER spent one cent there. I just stop in when I have to pee. No take-out ... only deposits, Sometimes I leave them a load of what I think of them. Put the strain on their plumbing. Try it; it's very satisfying.

And I'm telling you all this because for me, Waze had become the little app that cried wolf. Other Waze users, what for? Police? What police? Hazards? What hazards?" Until last night, on Route One.

"Hazard ahead!"

Pshaw, I say. I'm no fool. Step on it, Jacobs.

And then, dead ahead, I see colossal shards of rubber tires, maybe tractor tires, strewn over all three lanes. Now I'm swerving and dodging them like a dog on an agility track, barely missing the big mess and luckily making it past the actual hazard intact. Whew! Shaken, I pull off the road and watch other drivers skirting the debris, with some of them, finally, flinging much of the rubber rubble out of the way. Another driver who made it past the obstacle course pulls off the road, giving me a sympathetic eye roll as he parks on the shoulder in front of me. Clearly, we both need to calm down before going our own waze. And no, we did not hook up. At that point Waze was probably reporting the tire trash and us as hazards.

For once, I appreciated the heads up. And also, the report that there were six restaurants in the next two miles, all of which would serve me a cocktail.

With apologies to Billy Joel, I sang to the app, I love you just the waze you are.

NOVEMBER 2019

Funny About That . . .

I have a PTSD variant, Political Trauma Stress Disorder.

So, I've chosen *not* to write an angst-filled Fay's Year in Review column highlighting all the despicable lowlights of 2019. That would have been easy but depressing. Instead, I have chosen to recall things from the past year that made me smile, laugh out loud, or even tear up with happiness.

I flunked my sleep study. I was sent to a creepily quiet doctor's office at 7 p.m. one night and ushered into a tiny room with a bed, a TV, and a machine attached to about 100,000 wires and sensors. A half hour later, I was wearing all the wires and sensors like a prelit Christmas tree. "How am I going to sleep with all this crap attached to me? I'm the Bride of Frankenstein. There's no way I'm going to . . . z-z-z-z-z-z."

The technicians said I had the best night's sleep they'd ever witnessed. They could have gone out for pizza and not missed anything. I drove home before sunrise, laughing. Did you know Dunkin' Donuts at Midway opens at 5 a.m.?

At least my stomach doesn't brew its own beer. Can you believe the number of brewpubs popping up around here? But brewing's not just for brick and mortar anymore. I read about a man who was acting drunk but swore he was sober. Turns out his stomach was turning the carbs he ate into beer.

Apparently, the gut-wrenching truth is that "auto-brewery syndrome" is probably underdiagnosed. Are beach towns a disease cluster? Imagine being cited for driving under the influence of a sourdough sandwich.

I want my buzz to be from a Pomegranate Martini not a PB&J

Grey's Anatomy for Dogs. I love animal stories on TV. But

happy ones, I love seeing the Husky with the deformed front legs scooting around on his walker and rescued pets finding furever homes.

But watching animals with life-threatening diseases or injuries destroys me. I just cannot watch.

In fact, there are so many ninnies like me, who cannot stand to see animals in trouble, we have our own website called doesthedogdie.com. Seriously, it's a crowd-sourcing site where dog people warn other animal nuts if a fur baby is going to die in a movie or TV show. I've been known to bail six hours into a Netflix series if I get a "yes" after consulting doesthedogdie.com.

I don't want to watch vets trying to yank a gooey calf from the back end of a cow or operate on the swollen belly of a baby moose. My spouse watches this stuff and I cannot help bearing witness as I traverse to the kitchen. I beg her to change the channel, STAT!

Apparently, *My 600 lb. Life* wasn't real enough and now producers are giddily featuring my 600 lb. sow and her 16 lb. tumor and other animal grossities.

And, as with all reality TV, controversy and melodrama mean higher ratings. So now, real veterinarians are denouncing reality vets for over-dramatization. They worry that scripted excitement, ginned-up emergencies, and the need for cliff-hangers before commercials is leading to poor animal care.

And yes, I think I will be in better health if I stop watching sensationalized reality vets and go back to the equally unreal reality of HGTV's *Beach Front Bargain Hunting*. That's more like my happy place, watching with my dog on my lap, bonding for our mutual good health.

Those shows are just as bogus and scripted, but at least no animals were harmed in the making of this real estate deal.

Now if only the dog could get up and go make the popcorn.

So, this column is a milestone.

I've officially ended my twenty-fifth year writing this

column for *Letters from CAMP Rehoboth*. On to 2020 and more adventures. Wonder what kind of adventures 2020 will bring!

JANUARY 2020

Monster Land Yacht

The Queen Mary arrived in our driveway when our fourteen-year-old sedan died.

It's an enormous white 2014 SUV, a blend of the hospital ship Mercy and Moby Dick. It's so big (how big is it?) it makes the '05 Lexus SUV, also on our driveway, look like a Mini Cooper. And the seats in this behemoth can be configured to carry the entire New York Yankees starting lineup.

It barely held our luggage to Florida.

But, before we took off, we had to travel with it into the twenty-first century.

Here's the key. There wasn't one. Nothing that looked like a key, anyway. It took me weeks to stop reaching for a hunk of metal to stick in the ignition. Having my keys just hover on the passenger seat felt weird. And we'd never before had audio controls on the steering wheel, proportional power steering, and parking sensors in lieu of me shrieking "Stop!" Oh, and Bluetooth.

For the first couple of weeks, anytime my phone rang I'd try to answer but Bluetooth hijacked the call. My punching at the iPhone merely hung up on the hapless caller. "Hello? Hello?" It was Alexander Graham Bell screaming at Watson. We irritated our friends. I even hung up on a robo-call from the IRS threatening to jail me. *Ha-ha*.

One day, on my way to drop off the Lexus for service, I followed my spouse driving ahead of me in the Queen Mary. My iPhone rang and I answered it. But since I was stopped at a light behind Mother Mary, the call went to her Bluetooth. The caller and my wife chatted while I heard nothing. Of course, they had no idea who they were talking to and I had no idea what was happening.

When the light turned green and the Queen Mary pulled away, the call came back to me in time for the caller to hear "What the @#%$." Come here, Watson, I'm embarrassed.

The car is such a beast! I have yet to pull into a parking space without rolling over a curb or parking so close to an adjacent vehicle only Gumby can get out.

And then there was the incident at the car wash. Actually, it happened IN the car wash, midway between rinse and blow dry. The car battery died. The guys with the rags tried to get Elvis out of the building but it wouldn't start. They tried and tried, lifting the hood, fiddling with the battery, getting blown sideways and sucked dry as they worked.

Partially washed cars backed up; snarly patrons with still-dirty BMWs hollered "What's the hold-up?"; and of course, nobody could hear the answer for the screeching decibel level of the machinery. Then, the whole operation powered down with a sickening whoosh. Finally, a group of employees and bystanders pushed Biggie the Barge out onto the inclined pavement, where its sheer tonnage took over and it fled, stopping mere inches from mowing down the tip box. "Hey, Watson, call Triple A."

So, with an expensive new battery, off we went to drive a gaggle of women of a certain age around for a pub crawl. We proudly popped up that third bench seat in the back and three victims hopped in, our gang seeing no good reason to act our ages.

Turns out that freeing those three brave backseat gals from the Queen Mary was rather complex. Suffice it to say that exiting butt-first or alternatively butt-to-floor-to skootching out like a crab worked best, albeit accompanied by rude noises and an organ recital about knees and sciatica.

I will note that as the evening wore on, martini by daiquiri, entry and exit got easier. The designated driver reported that alcohol actually did grease the skids. But after that happy night, the back bench was off-limits to seniors and relegated to groceries and schnauzers.

So today was a milestone. I correctly answered a Bluetooth call on the first try ("No, Heather from Customer Service, I do not need an extended warranty"). I used the back-up camera to avoid both an errant grocery cart and the need for a chiropractor. And I pulled directly into a parking space without bouncing over the curb and destroying my rear alignment. Well, the Queen Mary's rear alignment. Mine's been shot for years.

And while I may have finally ridden the Queen Mary into the twenty-first century, not all is lost. There's still enough twentieth century hardware in her to plug in my ancient iPod and sing along to Springsteen's "Born to Run." Hashtag: GeezerOnWheels.

FEBRUARY 2020

At Least It's Not Corona

Well, I'm back for another year. There used to be a column in this magazine called Gay and Gray, written by a Rehoboth elder, retired to Florida. Good grief, is that now me?

Don't think so. First, I'm not giving up my crazy CAMPout adventures as I continue to refuse to act my age.

Besides, Gay and Gray wouldn't work. It would have to be called Gay and Foil with Two Percent Peroxide. I don't think my new editor would let that one go.

But if I wasn't secretly gray-haired anyway, I would have gone gray by this time, worried about a quickly spreading international pandemic as well as my own recent health crisis.

It started last fall when a physician's assistant in a cardiology office told me my heart was operating perfectly, but she saw high blood pressure in my lungs. I didn't even know lungs had blood pressure. She flippantly suggested I might have something called pulmonary hypertension. "Go see a pulmonologist."

First, of course, I hit Google and nearly lost my cookies. The Internet predicted my fairly quick decline into gasping, panting, oxygen tanks, and bye Felicia. No three-year Amazon Prime subscription for me. Good God.

So I frantically called for an appointment with a pulmonologist. It was October. "We can see a new patient in February."

"But I may have a fatal disease," I whined, and besides, "I'll be hyperventilating in Florida by then." Nobody cared.

So, I found a hotshot pulmonologist in Annapolis to see me the next week, where I spectacularly flunked my pulmonary function test. The doc asked, "Ever had asthma?"

"Yes, when I was a child."

And like Groucho Marx he wailed, "Well, you've got it again. "

Okay, then. Better news.

So, a few weeks later, in sunny Florida, I woke at 3 a.m. with a pain that seemed like an object the size of my head trying to pass through my right kidney. At the local ER they shot me full of morphine (lovely, by the way) and took pictures.

"You've got a large mass in your right lung."

Holy crap. Cue the *Phantom of the Opera* dirge. But the ER doc was great. "You'll never get a quick appointment here with a specialist, so I'm admitting you. We've got to find out what this is!"

So, I'm in a mini-hospital near my rental lodging, tended by a cadre of wonderful queer nurses, and wondering if I'll survive to get home in April. Amid three days of panic and Jell-O, I had two CT scans, a PET scan, and a needle biopsy, all trying to identify the blurry blob behind my boobs.

One morning I wake up, trying to contain a freak-out, when a frigging clown walks into my room. Could this get any worse? Frankly, he was dressed like some of the old coots you see in the street around here, but the big rubber nose gave him away.

"Hello," he giggles and proceeds to play a CD wailing Louis Armstrong singing "Hello, Dolly," while he makes me a balloon monkey. If I've died and this is hell, I am not surprised.

Mercifully, my doc comes in, dismisses the clown, and tells me I'm being sprung to worry at home for three days until we get biopsy results. Swell. We proceed with three days of uncomfortable conversations, cancer hospital research, talk about what ifs, and then I promise to write all the passwords down in one place. We eat, drink, and make as merry as possible, watching movies, cuddling with each other and Windsor.

Finally, with ants in our pants, we sit, waiting, in the doc's exam room. He bursts in the door, grinning, announcing, "You are one lucky woman! I was certain it was a tumor, but you have

...wait for it...pneumonia!"

And not just any pneumonia. I have something called BOOP. Seriously, BOOP. Bronchiolitis Obliterans Organizing Pneumonia. Very rare. Nonetheless, the good news is that it's not going to obliterans me. Nope, it's just something that's settled in for a long winter's nap, and something I need to take disgusting drugs to clear up. Whew!!! I have pneumonia. Yippee!!!!! BOOP BOOP Bi Do!

The fact is this disease is also called iBOOP, idiopathic BOOP, so now, along with my iPhone and iPad I have iBOOP. I'm so connected.

I probably developed it from bronchitis last fall—the symptoms my Rehoboth doc thought was the fatal lung disease, the Annapolis doc thought was asthma, and the clown thought warranted a balloon baboon.

So here's the deal. BOOP is a lot like what they used to call walking pneumonia. For the foreseeable future, I get to swallow a big dose of prednisone and keep getting CT scans to (hopefully) watch the big blob shrink. It's already down from giant schnauzer to a standard. Hoping for mini by April. And at least it's not that weird coronavirus thing running wild in Europe.

Of course, prednisone makes me pee like a racehorse, suffer hot flashes like I was fifty again, swim like a thirty-something (but hurt like a seventy-something the next morning), and continuously battle not to eat an entire package of Thin Mint Girl Scout Cookies.

But what the heck. I have pneumonia! I'm so happy! I hope it's gone when I get home in a few weeks. But even if not, whatever happens, don't send in the clowns. Don't bother, they're here.

MARCH, APRIL, MAY 2020

Pandemic Diary

Day One, Corona Incarceration, March 13

The country started to shut down this week. It's weird, it's frightening. It's a pandemic. No restaurants, no movies, no shopping. Very little toilet paper available. What to do for fun?

And a funny thing happened coming home to Rehoboth. I didn't. Being ancient and having just had pneumonia, we took no chances. So, I'm still in Florida, during what has now been called a pandemic We are sheltering in place.

And the place is a comfy house with a pool, plenty of food, booze, dog food, and our little pack ready for what comes next. But I'm homesick as hell.

The hoarding of toilet paper has begun. Luckily, there's a towering collection of coffee filters available. It could happen. It's all so 1918. Masks, newspaper updates, fear and loathing. Jeesh! This is really ugly, and I am terrified to step outside where other people and their germs may be lurking.

Day 15, Happy Thirty-Eighth F&B, March 27

Yes, it's our thirty-eighth anniversary, but Bonnie claims it's only nineteen as she only listens to me half the time.

Scored two enormous packages of toilet paper from a neighbor whose wife didn't like the brand he brought home. Who knew I'd ever be more excited about $50 worth of toilet paper than $50 worth of Grey Goose. Best anniversary gift ever.

For somebody who frequented restaurants regularly, even as a small child, I'm going cold turkey on eating out. I suspect I'll survive the withdrawal symptoms, but I have to remember not to tip Bonnie for my cold turkey sandwich.

Hey, we baked "special" brownies for dessert tonight.

Day 16, Alcatraz Daze, March 28

OMG, I haven't been that stoned since the Lyndon Johnson Administration. Happy anniversary!

Day 25. Cellblock Tango, April 6

Warrior pose! We do yoga three times a week with friends on FaceTime. And we walk to the marina, socially distancing from people and pelicans. We know how very lucky we are. We're retired, don't need to be anywhere in particular, and have everything we need. Our hearts hurt for those alone or suffering without food or jobs or money. And for those who have lost loved ones.

Day 28, Cloudy with a Chance of Boredom, April 9

So, the car gets three weeks to the gallon, but our grocery bill is the gross national product of Monaco.

TV sustains us with many reporters and interviewees working from home alongside their same-sex partners. With not a moment's hesitation we hear ". . . from Seth Doan and his husband, quarantined in Italy." It's grand progress no matter what the dolts in DC wish for us.

And today we lost a lesbian pioneer: Phyllis Lyon, wife of the late Del Martin, age 95 (natural causes). They started the first lesbian organization in the country, back in the 1960s. We stand on their shoulders for just about everything. RIP, brave Phyllis.

Day 32, In the Gulag, April 13

The Florida governor is opening the beaches. I guess folks want to look tan and healthy in their coffins. We are out of control, eating from boredom. I wear a mask outside to protect myself and others. I wear it inside the house to protect the Oreo stash.

Day 41, Gulfport Minimum Security Women's Prison, April 21

OMG, the morons! Terrorists, armed and dangerous, are protesting the stay-at-home orders and yelling "give me freedom or give me death." Who am I to tell them it's not either/or?

No matter what the governors decide, I'm staying hunkered down. Why risk death for a cut and color? I've said, "I'd rather die" than go gray, but clearly I didn't mean it.

Day 43, Just a Spoonful of Clorox®, April 23

Today Potus suggested getting disinfectant into our bodies so it would cure coronavirus the way it rids germs in the sink. There are people who will do this and die! I cannot fathom the stupidity involved in this suggestion.

But the ice cream man came down our street today. We bought Fudgsicles, handing over a $20 bill. Bonnie took the change in her gloved hand and after we had our treats, she washed the five and some ones with bleach. The drug cartels have nothing on our money laundering operation.

Day 44, 525,600 minutes... April 24

We had a full day of thunder and lightning, binged Netflix with *Circus of Books*, a fascinating look at a clueless heterosexual Jewish couple who wound up running the largest gay porn store in LA. Then we watched *A Secret Love*. It's a magnificent, heartbreaking story of two women who were together, closeted, for over seventy years. A must see.

Made mojitos with rum, simple syrup, and mint. We did not top it off with a disinfectant floater.

Day 51, The More Things Change, the More They... May 2

We send heartfelt thanks to essential business workers and medical staffs. We appreciate them more than we can show right now. They say the final death toll will be about one percent. To my mind it's going to take out the wrong one percent.

We get up early every morning to watch New York's Governor Andrew Cuomo talk sense about pandemic safety. Now there's a good leader. *(editor's note: "oy!")*

Day 59, May Day! May Day! (Deadline), May 10

By the time you read this, places are about to open. Please stay safe and skip the OxiClean™ martini. Don't touch your face. Whisper of how I'm yearning to mingle with the old-time throng. Give my regards to . . .

I'm heading home, vowing to disinfect myself regularly, only dine from drive-in windows, use public restrooms as infrequently as possible, and pray for the best. See you on FaceTime soon.

MAY 2020

Vanity Fare

"As long as we're spending so much time at home, we might as well spruce it up a bit."

I don't remember which one of us said it first, but it caused eight weeks of tile, caulk, construction rubble, and abject chaos. On a strict budget.

I bet many readers did this earlier in the quarantine, but we were imprisoned in Florida at somebody else's home, helping with *their* projects. Frustrating.

So, we started Project Update late, around June 1.

The guest bathroom was always merely adequate. Bright paint, a good shower curtain, and fun art helped disguise the butt-ugly vinyl floor, cheesy vanity, 1980s faucet, and mostly hidden but truly hideous beige tub in the otherwise white room.

So, Bonnie found a product to change any color tub and surround to a "new" bright white. But she had to do a dog and pony show to convince me to spend $250 on a bucket of goop. I caved after researching the cost of a new tub.

She applied the stuff like paint, but it was more like hot marshmallow oozing down the walls and tub. But like magic, it spread like a lava flow over the surface, covering every speck of repulsive beige. It looks great and you'd need a jeweler's loupe to see any flaws.

Next, water turned off (age carries the benefit of unfortunate experience), my spouse wrestled the vanity from its pipes, then unscrewed the toilet and dragged it to the guest room.

Bonnie tiled the floor like a pro, especially since we purchased plenty of extra tiles to cover, as Shakespeare wrote, the unkindest cuts of all. In all, she spent less time tiling than trying to get up off the floor when she was done.

But did we want another eighteen-inch vanity or a roomier twenty-four-inch? I needed to sit on the toilet to gauge required thigh room. But of course, the toilet was lying in the guest room, a fallen warhorse.

So, I squatted to a seated position where the toilet should have been and measured the distance from my thighs to where the twenty-four-inch vanity would end. Before I tipped over, I determined we'd be okay unless this stay home eating and drinking thing lasts more than another year.

Vanity, thy name is Amazon. And Wayfair, and Overstock. Thousands to choose from. And faucets and light fixtures and shower heads, and the UPS guy is now part of our quarantine bubble.

My design choices were mostly form over function, but entirely determined in the end by price. Luckily, there's lots of great design out there for cheap.

But I did not want to die on NobHill.com and it was a real possibility. After viewing thousands of choices, I almost ordered schnauzer knobs for the vanity. I fought the urge, going with contemporary brushed aluminum instead. It was close.

Then to reinstall the toilet. It took both of us to haul it back into place, but setting it on the two tiny screws on the ring eluded us. Bonnie directed me to lie face down on the floor, where I could see the new tile really up close and guide the porcelain horse into place while she held it up inches from my head. Love means never having to say "$^&*)*&%#$ the toilet's on my hand!" No broken bones and the new bathroom looks grand.

Next up, exterior work, painting the dingy maroon shutters black and the porch gray for a fresh look. Bonnie removed the shutters, then handed me a can of black paint and a paint brush. Moi??? This was serious. My princess card could be in jeopardy.

Twenty minutes later, as I labored in the hot sun, painting all the freakin' slats on the first of 10 shutters, Bonnie came to take a look.

"I have one question," I said.

"Yes?"

"How much do black shutters cost?" She ignored me.

The rest of our sprucing up included painting the front door and replacing a couple of light fixtures. Oh, and raising our rainbow flag on the porch.

That's it for now. The next house we want to improve is that white one on Pennsylvania Avenue in DC. As we turn to that task, we need to remove the ugly orange fixture and replace it with one with much better form and enormously improved function.

Let's work hard so that on January 20 we can send the new occupant a housewarming gift. I know just where to get German shepherd drawer pulls.

JUNE 2020

Out in the Fresh Air

Sometime during our confinement, thinking we'd be okay outside, away from germs, we rented a boat with some friends.

We met our first challenge renting the boat. Handed an iPad, we had to read all the horrid things that could happen to us or the boat for which the rental company would not be responsible. I hate any activity where you have to sign a waiver.

Worse, the iPad snapped our photos as we each signed consent. Nobody looks good after reading about their possible drowning. And I was surprised the screen fit all my chins.

"Why do they need our pictures?" asked one of our crew.

"To identify the bodies," somebody surmised.

Next, our octet of women of a certain age stepped carefully onto the boat. Then, we produced more tubes of sunscreen than are stocked at Walgreen's. We couldn't cast off until each of us looked like a pasty-faced mime.

And the clothing! Years ago, it was a bathing suit and a visor. Now, despite sunshine and 77 degrees, it was sweatshirts, long sleeves, and long pants. Only Captain Bonnie wore a bathing suit under her shorts and T-shirt. From the looks of it, the rest of us were going ice fishing.

We used to bring beer and chips. Now we stowed fat-free pretzels, gluten-free veggie chips, sugar-free flavored water, and caffeine-free Coke. Frankly, I thought this group could use some caffeine.

So, you should know that once upon a time, we were serious boaters. Without a shred of trepidation, we crossed Delaware Bay in a twenty-eight-foot cruiser, came out of Cape May into the ocean, hung a left, and cruised up to New York City, then Fire Island. We even lived on our boat on Rehoboth Bay, braved rough seas, and traveled the Intercoastal Waterway. We were foolish, fearless and without adequate sunscreen.

We thought we were those same people. Once underway the wind picked up, making for a choppy but fun ride. Face it, a pontoon boat is a floating great room—a little unwieldy to steer but by and large a sweet ride. We marveled at mansions on the water, dive-bombing pelicans, and way too many docks flying Trump flags. Yuk.

Deciding to anchor off a deserted beach seemed a good choice. I tossed the anchor out, feeling a pinch in my rotator cuff, and marveling at how much heavier the chunk of metal was than anchors of old.

As the metal device tried to take hold, the wind caught our floating hospitality suite and carried us directly over the settling anchor. Uh-oh, now twenty-five feet of anchor line (that's rope to you non-boaters) wrapped itself around the propeller.

I flashed back to the staggering amount our pre-cruise paperwork said it would cost us if we damaged the prop and glared glumly at the captain. "Okay, I can fix this," she said, shutting the engine down, flinging off her shorts and T-shirt, and scampering down the swim ladder into the water.

The aghast peanut gallery put down their flavored waters, moved to the rear of the boat, and stared at the captain, now hanging onto the motor like a Cirque du Soleil performer. She began unraveling the anchor line from the prop.

"Is it freezing?" asked a bundled-up passenger.

"I can't believe she went in!" said another.

"Glad it's not me," thought everybody else.

Whereupon the AARP audience cheered as the captain expertly freed the prop from the anchor line, causing nary a scratch to the machinery, then scampered back up into the boat. We all agreed that none of us would have willingly splashed down, and in fact we were not sure any of us were even capable of scaling the ladder back up into the boat.

I flashed back to the 1980s and '90s, a period I refer to as "my life as ballast," doing all the crazy things required to live on a boat, dock a boat, and otherwise athletically leap onto piers and jump up and down on the bow pulpit to free us from sandbars.

We've come a long way baby, into a new century, on dry land, and abject geezerhood.

But Captain Bonnie? Still crazy after all these years. Yay.

JUNE 2020

Truth Unmasked

Okay, readers, how's that social distancing and home quarantine going?

Like me, you probably have quarantine fatigue, are trying to make the best of it, and stave off permanent consequences. When this is over, I do not want to be invited on *My 600 lb. Life*. But it's dangerous when I find myself snacking on things I haven't eaten since Jimmy Carter was president.

It's hard being a comic writer when there's no inspiration. Most of my days are exactly the same. I do know there are people and things I've often said I wouldn't touch with a ten-foot pole. And now it's mandated government policy.

Hey, here's a Covid scoop. The half-century-old piercing in my left ear lobe closed up. We'd decided to "dress" for dinner in our own dining room one night just for the heck of it and discovered this news. For months now, earrings seemed extraneous with pajamas and yoga pants. But now I'll have to re-create that scene from *Grease* where we numb my ear with an ice cube, my spouse stabs a needle through my lobe, and we both sing "Look at me, I'm Sandra Dee."

This afternoon, something different happened. We heard the tinny sound of Scott Joplin music and saw the ice cream man come down the street. Yay!!!! We socially distanced with the proprietor as he lobbed us the Fudgsicles, collected our cash with salad tongs, and returned to us the change the same way. Then we ran to the sink to wash off the wrappers.

Let's see, what else? Oh yeah, I've been riding my adult tricycle in the neighborhood. As I pedal around waving to the neighbors I can't tell if I'm Jessica Fletcher looking for a murder to solve or Margaret Hamilton spitting "And your little dog, too!"

And my little dog too is going a bit nuts. I'm dragging him out for more walks than he wants. I think he's praying we go out more and leave him home to chew his tail in privacy.

So here we are. Same #*&#@ different day. How I hope as you read this life has seeped back to a more normal scenario. I'm pretty sure it won't ever be back to the way we were (cue Streisand), but maybe that's okay.

I hope our coastal businesses survive and employees go back to work and paychecks. I hope fewer people are getting ill and the flood of tragedy has been stemmed. But I also hope we appreciate and compensate our essential workers more, understand how we must protect folks in nursing homes and in the food chain, and take some time to appreciate the human connections we've missed so terribly while hunkering down at home.

See, I told you it was a tough time to be a humorist. But I'm rallying. I just got back from the bathroom, and guess what? I got high score on the scale today. Look out, Oreos.

JUNE 2020

Pride in June, Pride Year-Round

Often, many of us from the beach and its burbs can't quite verbalize what makes this community so special. LGBTQ welcoming, for sure. Also, the sophisticated culinary scene, the work of CAMP Rehoboth, our dedication to the arts, and a million little ways in which thousands of people, LGBTQ and straight alike, feel safe and supported as they live, work, and visit here.

But if there's one story exemplifying our culture of supporting each other, it's the story of Joe and Darryl, longtime Rehoboth business owners and residents. They tangled with COVID-19 over the past three months, and without any intention of doing so, showed us all the reasons why we have such tremendous pride in our community.

The public saga started with a three-word a Facebook post on March 29: "Please PRAY today."

But the story started days before as Joe, in Mexico at the time, learned that Darryl, back home in Rehoboth, was sick, probably with COVID-19. They spoke several times daily, about Darryl's symptoms, the doctor's advice, and finally, when things got really bad, with Joe staying on the phone as Darryl drove himself to the hospital on March 29.

From the emergency room, Darryl told Joe they'd probably take his phone, so they said their goodbyes. Darryl said, "I'll talk to you as soon as I can."

That turned out to be forty days later.

Still in Mexico, Joe talked to Darryl's doctor, who asked what the two men's relationship was—married? Boyfriends? Friends? "He wanted to be sure to address us properly," Joe said, and told the doctor that Darryl was his husband.

Then, the doctor asked Joe's permission to put Darryl on a ventilator.

"When I hesitated, the doctor said, 'Sir, your husband is in very critical condition. He may not be alive in thirty minutes unless we do something.'" The doctor also asked Joe if the hospital could call clergy if last rites were needed.

Joe gave permission for both the ventilator and the clergy.

And as his flight home from Mexico was ready to board, Joe posted those three words: "Please PRAY today."

By the time Joe landed in LA for his connection, there were twenty-five messages with prayers and hugs on his Facebook account; by Philly the number had leapt to over 150. The two flights, with frustrating delays, were "the longest thirteen hours I have ever spent," Joe says. But while he was in airplane mode silence, Facebook exploded with family, friends, acquaintances, and customers sending prayers, healing energy, positive vibes, and a whole litany of good wishes.

Darryl was in very critical condition, sedated, breathing with a ventilator, and connected to a network of tubes and monitors as Joe spoke with doctors, chaplains, and support staff.

"Darryl is such a private person," Joe says. "I didn't know what he'd think of my telling everyone what was going on, but so many people wanted to know." So many that daily Facebook reactions, those little hearts, thumbs up, crying emojis, etc., approached 400, with another 160 daily comments. This was a massive neighborhood watch.

People sent Joe posts of hope, optimism, healing light, and a thousand warm, sincere messages of support. There were added prayers on Good Friday and Passover, and then Easter, with hundreds of Facebook posts every single day, plus calls and texts and whatever else people could think of doing to help.

Two weeks into the nightmare, Joe wrote "I am continually honored and touched on the ongoing support we have—many BLESSINGS . . . Happy Easter" he told Facebookers, announcing he finally saw which room Darryl was in and could stand outside and look up at the window. A nurse put a speaker phone in the room so Joe's comatose husband might be able to hear his voice.

One morning Joe wrote "The care is over the top with compassion and professionalism," continuing, "And yes," Joe said, responding to pleas that he take care of himself, "Yes, I do sleep and eat—I am good—know you are worried. I AM OK!"

He was also much more than merely okay with the hospital staff, with everyone from phone operators to nurses and doctors asking Joe how his husband was doing. Yes, *using the word husband*. This level of sensitivity at a place where twenty years ago, many of us, me included, encountered rampant homophobia and disrespect as our partners received care, was rewarding. This wholesale change is a tangible sign of the success our community has achieved and the bridges we have built by working together for equality.

But then came a cascade of terrifying complications. As medical staff tried to wean Darryl from sedation and oxygen, he got pneumonia and a temperature spike to an unimaginable 107 degrees, plus blood clots, a low platelet count, and the need for transfusions. Hospital staff was up to the horrific challenge.

It was a rollercoaster of good news, then frightening setbacks. A trach was placed in Darryl's airway; his COVID-19 test was negative but other issues clouded that report. He remained critical but stable, sedated, and comatose, with blood clots and other complications. Joe began calling for a miracle.

The community hovered in unison, praying, and waiting, for over a month. Restaurants and CAMP Rehoboth fed the medical team at the hospital while continued thoughts, hugs, prayers, love, hearts, and rainbows came pouring in—now closing in on 500 daily Facebook reactions and hundreds more daily comments. The whole community, thousands of people, checked in daily to wait for better news.

Finally, it happened. Sedation reduced, Darryl was waking up and the ventilator was doing less of his breathing. Nurses and therapists had him up in a chair, starting to assess his memory and cognitive function. They had him doing leg lifts, arm lifts, and exercise to regain his strength.

Virtual cheers by the thousands went up online when the team got Darryl up and walking. Joe posted "I CAN NOT THANK each of you for all the phone calls, text messages . . . PRAYERS from every religion and over and above all the LOVE and SUPPORT we are getting. We are SO BLESSED to have you with us."

And on April 25, "One month . . . 672 hours . . . 40,320 minutes . . ." said Joe, there was FaceTime contact. Darryl couldn't talk because of the trach, but he managed to communicate "Where are you?" Joe told him he was at the bar they owned, and Darryl cried.

He didn't yet understand why Joe couldn't visit, or exactly what had happened in the previous month, but things continued to improve, despite ongoing pneumonia, infections, and blood clots.

Joe wrote "After 34 days in ICU, Darryl was finally moved to a Step-Down room. I can never thank the ICU TEAM ENOUGH for saving my Darryl's life so many times. All of you who sent messages, Your Prayers, Thoughts, Positive vibes all EMBRACED and supported both of us. YOU are . . . a HUGE part of our survival . . . BLESS YOU . . ."

Finally, Joe could visit Darryl on iPad FaceTime, and plans came together to transfer the patient to a rehab facility. On day forty of this Covid nightmare, as he left for rehab, Joe reported that Darryl was learning to speak with the trach, learning to swallow and eat food again, and anxious to do the work needed to come home. "The best news!" Joe heralded, "His brain is working!!!"

And that day's good news was viewed by 637 people

reacting with available emojis and another 357 people adding joyous comments. The daily Facebook check-ins were heading toward 1,000.

And in a marvelous, moving outpouring of well wishes and support, just before Memorial Day, when Darryl came home, neighbors organized a drive-by auto parade of honking, cheering, and applause for the couple who stood outside their home watching and waving.

The drive-by video was posted on Facebook. I pushed play and burst into tears—happiness for my friends Joe and Darryl, and a flood of emotion for our community.

In this pandemic, so many have been alone, but together, in love and support for those needing help—supporting our restaurants with carry-out, honoring our first responders, donating to feed and support medical staffs, doing Zoom support groups, and communicating online or by phone. Clearly, we cannot keep our community from gathering, socially distanced and masked or online, and supporting one another.

And we now have a big, happy story to help explain to outsiders our pride for our Delaware beach community. We are who we are, and it's pretty great.

JULY 2020

Demolished: A Wild Gay History

A little piece of Rehoboth's gay history disappeared in these last few weeks. The famed Carpenter mansion, on the beach behind Silver Lake and adjacent to Poodle Beach at the south end of the boardwalk, has been demolished. I'm heartbroken.

Officially called The Shell House, lore has it that the mansion, formerly a DuPont property, was where Rehoboth's LGBTQ life really began.

Outrageous actress Tallulah Bankhead, who rented a Rehoboth summer house, once frolicked at the mansion with her dear friend, DuPont heiress Louisa D' Andelot Carpenter. Louisa spent a lot of time at the beach house, originally built by her parents in the early twentieth century. The house itself was an enormous shingled "beach cottage," situated behind protective dunes, facing the ocean.

Louisa hunted fox and pheasant and was the first woman master-of-hounds in America. She would become one of the first licensed women pilots as well.

While Louisa was married to DuPont executive John Lord King Jenney in 1929, it was open knowledge that the socialite and aviatrix was interested in Sapphic romance. The marriage ended quickly.

As early as the 1920s and well into the 1950s, Tallulah brought her Broadway and Hollywood pals like singer Libby Holman, playwright Noel Coward, and movie star Greta Garbo to party with Louisa at the beautiful home on the ocean. And Louisa kept company with several well-known lesbians, including Marion "Joe" Carstairs, a Standard Oil heiress who cross-dressed, raced speed boats, and sported tattoos.

Newspaper stories reported that Louisa and her string of

lovers, one of them Tallulah's sister, gathered at the beach house for years. But it was torch singer Libby Holman who captured Louisa's attentions.

My pal Rich Barnett found a June 11, 1937, announcement in the *Delaware Coast Press* reporting Libby Holman "arriving at Rehoboth by plane on Wednesday evening and staying at the home of Mr. and Mrs. R.M.M. Carpenter near Silver Lake."

Historian Elisa Rolle writes in *Days of Love*, "Their affair . . . became well-known and, for the most part, accepted within both society and theatre circles. One of Libby's actress friends fondly referred to Louisa as "he-she" because of Louisa's fondness for hunting and men's clothing."

But in 1931, Libby married Smith Reynolds, the North Carolina heir to the Reynolds tobacco fortune. The marriage was combative, with Louisa as a frequent house guest, dressed always in masculine attire and enjoying bootleg champagne. It became a love triangle leading to Rehoboth's Louisa Carpenter getting involved in a scandalous murder mystery.

At a drunken party on July 4, 1932, Libby and Smith argued amid lots of drinking, disrobing of guests, and other shenanigans. When a shot was heard from the bedroom, guests found Reynolds dead from a gunshot to the head. Suicide or murder? The authorities ruled suicide at first, but then a grand jury charged Libby with murder. Louisa Carpenter paid her $25,000 bail.

While the charges were eventually dropped, and the case never solved, the scandal was all over the newspapers as one of the biggest stories of the year. Libby and Louisa quietly returned to Delaware.

Rolle writes, "Their 'Boston marriage' was widely known and accepted. And the two women were often photographed with matching bobbed haircuts, tennis whites, and deep tans— like adolescent country club boys, someone commented."

The relationship continued through the 1950s when Libby

returned to the stage. Louisa stayed in Delaware and on a farm near Easton, Maryland, as well as a home in Florida. In 1971, Libby Holman committed suicide, the mystery of Reynold's death never unraveled.

Through the mid-1970s, Louisa could be seen entertaining at the Carpenter mansion and on the beach in front of her home. In 1976 she died, piloting her own plane to a crash landing in Easton. She was 68.

Throughout the decades, as more gay people vacationed in Rehoboth, the beach next to the mansion was dubbed Carpenter Beach, the unofficial "gay beach." The gathering spot moved north by a few blocks when the gay people sunbathing there wanted to be closer to Rehoboth's boardwalk refreshments.

It was a very short walk from the end of the Rehoboth boardwalk to the mansion, and back in the mid-'90s lots of us trekked over to see the enormous home.

Over the years, the family sold off portions of the original lot, with huge, contemporary beach homes now facing the ocean. According to an article about a year ago in the *Cape Gazette*, the property was owned by the DuPont family until around 2000. Most recently it was listed for sale at $14.9 million.

And now it's gone, a piece of Rehoboth's queer history lost to demolition. Louisa and Libby would be appalled. I'd like to think that somewhere they are toasting to the good times with bootleg champagne.

JULY 2020

Home in the Time of Covid

My home, you may recall from previous columns, is a mobile a.k.a. manufactured home or, if you must, a trailer. Although I think of my community as the "Greenwich, Connecticut, of trailer parks."

And, like almost everybody else these days, we've been fixing up the place. Spend enough time at home and you notice that the bathroom vanity may have come over on the Mayflower. Likewise, the 1980s called and they want their porch rails back. That is, if you can get new contemporary railing spindles.

In renovating we've discovered that some products, formerly easily obtainable, are now as scarce as hen's teeth. In fact, like hen's teeth, these products, at least in July when I am penning this, are nonexistent phenomena.

In fact, I'd trade a whole set of hen's teeth made on a 3-D printer for the out-of-stock railing spindles. Which reminds me, did you know that KFC experimented with chicken nuggets on a 3-D printer using lab-grown chicken? I'd rather eat railing spindles. But I digress.

Working outside on the porch in the blistering heat made me long for a three-ring inflatable baby pool. You cannot get a baby pool. Anywhere. Orders are backed up like Route One on a Saturday in August. Given the heat, what I'd give (3-D printed nuggets?) for a refreshing dunk in some cold water. But no. Baby pools are gone.

They're in backyards of clairvoyant families who, back in April, thought "come June and July, we'll still be here at the house, the community pool will be too dangerous, so let's order a three-ring kiddie pool now."

Would that have been me. But it wasn't. And now they are

out of stock everywhere.

So, I convinced myself that due to Covid, I really deserved a thousand-jet five-person octagonal hot tub. For now, we could keep it as cool as a pool and have a private dunk tank.

Just try and find one. Hot tubs, formerly hawked at convention center or fairground home shows, with competing salespeople shouting like circus barkers and offering incentives, are back ordered for eight months.

And woe is me if I wanted an elliptical trainer or squat-assist row and ride exercise equipment, which as you must know I don't. But now, that stuff, formerly used in many homes merely as towel racks, is suddenly a hot commodity, back-ordered as well.

Know what else you can't buy? An RV. Covid-quarantined families are snapping up RVs to have their own germ-free beds, kitchens and toilets, thereby saving their vacation plans.

We used to stop by dozens of RV dealers to ogle RVs, and before we could even see a vehicle, we'd have to give name, address, serial number and Medicare card. For months on end there would be badgering follow-up calls, notes, and emails from hungry salespeople. It was years before we fell off the birthday card list. Now, they've no time to talk and hardly an RV left to sell.

And hey, real estate seekers, don't let those listings linger. We may be having a Covid-caused economic turndown, but here in the coastal region it hasn't hit real estate. Given all the stay-at-home advice, lots of folks want to stay home in a new one. My Realtor friends are happy.

But I have to say, the most shocking backorder and product shortage I've noticed (since the great March 2020 run on toilet tissue) is the disappearance from grocery shelves of humble microwave popcorn. Back-ordered, baby.

I guess It was inevitable, what with all the Netflix, Amazon, and CNN binging going on as people hunker down with home entertainment to avoid the perils of the pandemic. And what's a good movie without popcorn? Last night I had to find out. It was, well, lacking in crunch.

I'm calling KFC. The heck with lab-grown chicken nuggets on a 3-D printer. Make me some 3-D Orville's butter-flavored popcorn. While waiting for my baby pool. It's all I need right now at Home Sweet Mobile.

JULY 2020

Check the Spaghetti Model

I was furious, quick, and didn't do too much damage. Thankfully.

Of course, I'm talking about my namesake, Tropical Storm Fay. Although for about twelve hours here at the beach we got drenched and deluged, followed by some pretty bad flooding.

In our neighborhood, kids actually boogey-boarded in the streets. I hope the flooding wasn't too severe elsewhere.

But for me, having lived with a fairly uncommon first name all these years, this was kind of fun. I had twenty-four hours of headlines screaming my name, spelled correctly for once, in 40pt type. Television graphics had me crawling along the bottom of the screen with viewers following my path.

Weather forecasters added scary music and hyperventilating warnings about Fay.

As it happened, the storm formed off the North Carolina coast and moved north, eventually making landfall near New York City.

Under Covid conditions, this was the only way I'd get to see Manhattan this summer. I hope the storm had a knish for me.

And according to reports, Fay was notable as the earliest "F" storm or sixth-named such storm recorded—beating out 2005's Tropical Storm Franklin by over a week. The "F" storms historically haven't arrived until early September.

It makes sense, as this Fay is pathologically early. If I'm merely on time, people have already considered calling the hospitals. I often arrive at airports before ticketing counters open, in case the plane takes off ahead of schedule. I drive my wife nuts. So, to have Fay, the storm, the F-bomb, arrive early was not a shock.

From July 9 to July 12, every time I turned around somebody

had something to say about me. When they announced, "Fay has become better organized," I thought yeah, have you seen my desk?

"Fay has picked up strength and speed," said nobody about me, ever.

Although when they talked of "maximum sustained winds increasing to 60 mph, with higher gusts," I'm sure Bonnie had flashbacks to some of our fiercest conversations.

As I continued to pummel the coast and cause sideways rain here at the beach, I was amused when Hugh from the Purple Parrott posted on Facebook, "Due to Fay throwing a tantrum today, we will only be open for take-out."

He actually had somebody comment "What did Jacobs do to you?"

Then Facebook comments revved up. "Go away, Fay!" "I always knew you were a badass," and when I asked if I'd be trouble, the answer was "no more than usual."

I did enjoy what the forecasters called the Spaghetti Models. That's where they chart a storm's many possible paths and the resulting map looks like it's covered with spaghetti.

I was educated about a previous Tropical Storm Fay in 2008 (what was I up to that I don't recall this?) when the storm hit Florida on four different passes, turning the Spaghetti Model into corkscrew fusilli.

But for this storm, I was quite proud that not one of the models showed Fay's touchdown in New Hampshire, and yet, the unctuous orange oligarch in the White House canceled a campaign speech there due to ME! I waved my Fay Pride flag.

The whole thing reminded me of minor Hurricane Bonnie in 1996, when we hunkered down for the storm on our boat and then got T-shirts saying, "I survived Hurricane Bonnie." Tropical Storm Fay wasn't around long enough for immortalization on an item of clothing. But I wore that "I survived Hurricane Bonnie" T-shirt for years.

So Tropical Storm Fay provided me with some Covid diversion. Especially since I heard of no loss of life and not too much property damage. It was amusing to see the headlines shrieking my name and saying completely inappropriate, incongruous things about me. It was a silly good time.

Of course, all good (or at least distracting) things come to an end, and after making landfall I "degenerated into a *post-tropical depression.*"

Nothing a little Grey Goose couldn't cure—because in true namesake fashion, Tropical Storm Fay cleared up completely, just in time for a sunny, dry (or in my case, extra-dry) martini happy hour.

SEPTEMBER 2020

Thanks for the Memories

So, I've been asked by my book publisher to write a memoir. Methinks she's anxious for me to do it now while I have some of my memory stick left. Does she know something I don't? And frankly, what else did I have to do in Covid quarantine?

But what is "writing a memoir"? Is it a ponderous whole-life autobiography designed to send readers into REM sleep? Is it a highlight reel of my humor career? Or social activism? Is it a bit of all of it?

So, I started writing.

Page one. I was born. Oh yeah, that's when my father was outside the hospital listening to a Yankee game on the radio in the 1948 Buick and missed the whole event. Which pretty much summed up our entire relationship.

Soon I slid down the rabbit hole, recalling my parents hope to cure my tomboy tendencies by sending me to ballet class. I was consistently a step and a half behind the other tutu-clad ballerinas. Our Kodak moments from the recitals hilariously prove it. I laugh now, but it was arabesque torture.

Moving along, I write about my religious training, which consisted mostly of eating lox and bagels and attending the rare religious service. I do recall a holiday costume party where my sister and I went as the Torah. It was not a well-developed plan. We wrapped ourselves in several sheets, stapled together and rolled ourselves up, face to face.

Sadly, the sheets were so tight we couldn't bend to get in the car and had to be loaded into the back of the station wagon like cargo. We lay there, rolled up like carpet remnants, snickering. On the whole, it was a hint I shouldn't pursue a career in costuming.

Fall 1964, my sister and I enrolled in The Rhodes Prep School, a private senior high located in two enormous Georgian townhouses just down the block from our New York apartment. It was the school used by J.D. Salinger as his model for *Catcher in the Rye*.

From what I could tell, Rhodes was made up of some professional kids, like young Broadway and TV performers, other students whose parents didn't want them in city high schools, kids like us who lived up the block, and offspring of people who waited for their kids after school in big black limos with blacked out windows. A lot of my classmates had fathers who dressed like funeral directors and ran import/export or liquor distribution businesses. Hmmm.

Eight weeks into this writing exercise I got to the day I left for college. Exiting New York and heading to Washington, DC, I was all Revlon makeup, false eyelashes, stockings with garter belts, girdles (yes, we all wore them then), ladylike Villager-brand clothing, and Bass-Weejuns penny loafers.

Within three months, after making friends in the theater department and the dorm, I shed it all for ratty bell bottoms, a headband, tie-dyed shirts, Birkenstock sandals, and no brassiere. I did everything but go to San Francisco with flowers in my hair. And my folks got a Thanksgiving surprise.

I also looked back on my college years marching against the Vietnam War, with my head sticking through the moon roof in a 1965 VW Bug, at the Lincoln Memorial, taking photos with a heavy Nikon. And marching for the ERA, idolizing Bella Abzug and Gloria Steinem, working for Robert Kennedy, my hero, in my first-ever political campaign and being devastated by the assassinations of RFK and Martin Luther King Jr.

I was on the scene at the DC District Building while the city burned, trying to help people find milk and diapers for their babies. It was a heady time. Oh, and somehow, in between extracurricular activities and smoking pot, I got a journalism degree.

So, I've been working on this project since March, and I'm only up to age 31 and my leaping from the closet. Prior to my outing myself, my father had some advice for me: "It wouldn't kill you to wear a dress to your sister's wedding" and "You'll never find a husband if you buy a house with another girl." He was right on both counts.

Why am I giving away all the memories? Won't it cut down on my royalties on my way to a *New York Times* Best Seller? Well between you and me, I have absolutely no expectation of getting the damn thing finished.

So, what the heck. If I do keep going, I may have another installment in this series. So, take a bit of the journey with me. What else have we got to do in the Age of Covid?

AUGUST 2020

I Kissed a Penguin and I Liked It

Not recently, but heck, without too many adventures happening these Covid days, I have to write about something.

I first fell for penguins in the '90s at Sea World. I entered a penguin building and stepped on a conveyor belt walkway taking me past an enclosure with dozens of penguins frolicking, sliding into the water, and sipping saltwater drinks—just like my Saturdays at the beach.

Transfixed by the tuxedoed troupe, I traveled the moving pathway much like luggage at the airport. Then I exited, ran back around to the front and, went around again, an unclaimed suitcase. I was gob-smacked by these adorable creatures and kept going back for more. Finally, my wife ambushed me at the exit to prevent me from lapping the track a seventh time.

Back home I watched all eleven of the *New York Post's* "Greatest Penguin Performances in Film." My TV habits were so peculiar Netflix failed to come up with any "Because you liked . . ." suggestions.

Did you know that penguins waddle to raise their center of mass because they have such short legs? Perhaps I'm drawn to them by having something in common.

It was in 2014 that I was sure I'd get my personal penguin meet-up. We traveled over a thousand miles to the Galapagos Islands, where you can mingle freely with sea lions, Blue-Footed Boobies (seriously), tortoises, and Galapagos penguins. Visitors cannot emulate Diana Ross to reach out and touch somebody, but I did have a sea lion come up and sit on my foot. I hoped for a penguin incident.

But while thousands of adorable birds hung out on the rocky island shores, our inflatable craft could not get close enough for even a hand-to-flipper high five. Photos galore, but no touchy-feelies. Drat!

Finally, last March I had my bucket list experience. As Katy Perry inspired, I kissed a penguin, and I liked it. Actually, he kissed me. At the zoo in Tampa, Florida, I signed up for a close encounter of the feather kind, where a handful of zoo visitors sit in a courtyard enclosure with a Waddle (yup, not a flock or gaggle) of penguins.

We waited with "baited breath" for the birds with the fish breath. A door opened and six black and whites waddled forward in a line. I hummed the March of the Siamese Children from *The King and I*. They came toward us and the largest penguin—"That's Bolt," said the Naturalist—came directly to me and brushed up against my leg with his cheek, a penguin kiss. I melted. He did the kiss thing again, then he looked up, right into my adoring eyes, and pecked my arm with his sharp beak. "Ow!" I yipped.

"Bad boy, Bolt!" yelled the Naturalist, as a tiny drop of blood, my red badge of courage, appeared just above my wrist.

Immediately, I could see Bolt was remorseful, as he did the shin kiss again and just sat there, looking up adoringly at me. Love means never having to say you're sorry.

"Oh, my!" said the Naturalist. "He might be a little stressed. He's about to have his catastrophic molt where he'll lose, then replace, all his fur over the next two weeks."

"So right now, he's having pre-molt-stral mood swings? I asked.

"Yes," said the Naturalist, "but thankfully it's not monthly; it's just once a year!"

I stared at Bolt and then at the tiny scratch of red on my arm. "Face it," said my snarky companion," it's been a long time since you've been this close to a pecker."

Even Bolt laughed.

The Naturalist brought me a swab of alcohol to tend my

wound, and Bolt continued to hang with me for the encounter's remaining fifteen minutes. He rubbed my ankle a final time before he and his buds waddled away. Then I signed up to "adopt" Bolt with a donation for his continued care. Perhaps for anger management class.

But I have no regrets. Bolt and I are a bonded pair. I keep up with him in zoo newsletters and cannot wait for a return visit. In the meantime, I'm looking into importing penguins locally. I can build a backyard enclosure with a hard-scape and lap pool. Build it and they will come?

Oh, how I hope so. Somebody let Bolt know I'm working on the permits.

SEPTEMBER 2020

Hello, I'm Calling from the IRS

My fifth book was titled *Fried & Convicted*. Just a fun title, meaning nothing. But could that become my reality?

Last March the IRS contacted me last saying I owed them over $3,500 plus big fines and accumulating interest. They accused me of failing to report $60,000 in income in 2018. Failure to pay up could send me up the river to the Big House for tax evasion.

Whoa. Not only do I look terrible in orange, but trying to hide $60,000 in income would have required the Amazing Kreskin. In 2018 my entire freelance writing biz made only a fraction of that amount. I know, pathetic, isn't it? And the 1099 document they were citing reported my gargantuan earnings from a client as a mere $600.

So, this raised the $60,000 question. What $60,000?

Instantly, horror stories of the relentless IRS completely ruining innocent lives played in my head. People losing their homes, their careers, and their paychecks garnished. Do you also picture sliced lemons and limes when you hear about garnishing wages?

Or how about those commercials for companies paid handsomely to get the IRS off customer's backs? I'd watch those and cluck my tongue thinking the customers should have paid the tax in the first place. Now I feel awful. Maybe their wretched $600 in income was also turned into $60.000 by IRS auditor Mr. Magoo.

Okay, keep calm. How do you tell the IRS they've diddled with a decimal point, and their bean-counters perpetrated a ridiculous $59,400 error? I didn't want to be sarcastic, but I did want to tell them "You do the math."

Well, my accountant (laughing, but then serious) wrote to the IRS advising them of their insanely stupid mistake. Although he used a more professional thesaurus.

Then months went by as I obsessed about being sent to the Sussex County Correctional Center or to a federal minimum-security prison. Gee, I hope it would be minimum security, as I'm no Big Boo from *Orange Is the New Black*, capable of lugging $60,000 in pennies to a hiding place, then beating up the corrections staff before lunch.

Would I be treated like serial killer Ailene Wuornos (as played by my crush Charlize Theron), or suffer like Tim Robbins in *The Shawshank Redemption*, excavating the concrete prison wall with a spoon? Did he use an iced tea spoon or a soup spoon? Do people really hide shivs in cakes? Why do I even know the word shiv?

For months, my imagination ran wild. Then, when I had run out of prison films to obsess over and nightmare scenarios to envision, I finally got another letter from the IRS. They told me they had received my CPA's letter (good), and (wait for it) they'd decided nothing. Bupkis. Nada. It was still under review. By whom? A fourth-grader with arithmetic issues?

They'd used a postage stamp to tell me they'd done absolutely zip. But here's the kicker. If I thought I would owe them money when they finally did get around to making a decision, they warned me to pay up now because the clock was ticking on interest. Beasts!

I wrestled with what to do, but ultimately did not send them one more cent, though I'm sure they thought I had 59,999 more pennies stashed in my she-shed.

Time marched on, when finally, this morning, thanks to a 9 a.m. email from USPS Informed Delivery Service, I learned I would have an IRS letter in my mailbox today—at about 4 o'clock. Now ordinarily I don't mind this teasing service, but today it just made me nuts. Should I troll the area, hunting down my mailperson to hijack my delivery? Should I knock myself out for the next seven hours?

Well, finally, nearing cocktail hour the mail arrived. The official IRS missive said simply, "We are pleased to tell you that the information you provided resolved this tax issue. You owe $0.00 and this case is now closed." The good news was if they screwed with the decimal point this time, the amount owed would remain the same.

Wheeee! No fines. No interest. No jail. I'm going to pour myself a large cocktail. I may get good and fried, but at least I won't be convicted.

OCTOBER 2020

Cyber-Bullied

I was at my computer in my office, about to be the guest speaker on a Zoom program originating at an LGBTQ organization in Pennsylvania. I'd been asked to give my gay history program, *Gay with Fay, the History Nobody Taught You in School* and I was excited about the opportunity.

Spreading the word about gay history is a passion of mine. After all, I learned about my Jewish heritage and heroes from my parents at lox and bagels breakfasts. Likewise, I learned about liberal values and Democratic pioneers while stuffing envelopes with my parents for a primary candidate. When it became a subject of fledgling confusion for me, I was acutely aware that my parents had never said a single word about homosexuality, let alone its pioneers. I was on my own.

As a result, realizing that very few young queer kids have parents who can proudly pass along gay history, it became important for me to do so wherever I could.

Hence, I was sitting in my office, Covid quarantine in full swing, preparing to share an overview of gay history in the US.

As the moderator welcomed us, three more people joined. They wore MAGA hats, and began screaming vile things accompanied by ear-splitting sounds, film of a Klan cross-burning, with words, in all caps, pouring onto our chat screen: NO FAGS! NO NIGGERS! NO JEWS! Over and over, the hackers continued to scream disgusting things, their ugly, hate-filled faces taking up the whole computer screen, literally being in our faces. No fags, No N-word, No Jews, No lesbians. No liberals, No queers, it went on and on. It was a disgusting home invasion into my office through my computer.

It took seven interminable minutes to block these screaming, hate-spewing assholes. It felt personal, unexpected, like being blindsided. And it was one of the most terrifying incidents in my life as a writer, LGBT activist, and human being.

Luckily, once the Zoom was secured, the moderator asked if I wanted to go on with the program. I did. It was a little less humorous and relaxed than usual, but we got through it.

By the time I turned off the computer I realized I was shaking. When I told my wife what happened, I tried to hold back the tears and anger but lost the fight.

This morning, after a lousy night's sleep, much of my time still picturing those terrifying images, I went out the front door and took down our Pride flag. In the middle of the night, I'd remembered a haunting story from the '90s about a hater burning down the home of a lesbian couple. I thought about us and my dog Windsor. I didn't want trouble.

This afternoon, I heard that the organization presenting the hacked Zoom reported the incident to the police. It seems Zoombombing (yes, there's a name for it) is a federal crime.

These haters must feel emboldened by the Trump presidency even if it's now all over but the shouting – at least I hope so.

By later that morning, the community center in Pennsylvania posted a note about the incident on Facebook as did I. As it turned out there had been two other incidents of hatred the previous day as well.

An interracial lesbian couple I knew had five-foot letters spelling out TRUMP burned into their lawn with chemicals. In addition, the co-captain of a local fire department posted on Facebook that he'd been to a "faggot show" at a nearby gay bar.

This startling trifecta of bigotry was covered in the newspaper and on our NPR station, and our own gay community center reached out to me, the two women with the destroyed lawn, and the beloved local drag queen who had been called the derogatory name. When I was interviewed on NPR, I told them I took the Pride flag off the porch in an abundance of caution.

And while the incidents made me sick and angry, the friends and neighbors who read about the crime responded to us all and made up for it. "Stay strong!" "Sorry, this happened." "We're behind you. "Don't give up the fight" and a flood of supportive emails too many to mention.

My neighbor, a straight older gentleman, knocked on our door and asked my wife Bonnie how I was doing. "And if she won't put that flag up, I'll put it up at my house."

I was moved by his offer.

I gathered myself, put the incident in perspective, and by 4:30 that afternoon I went back outside to raise the Pride flag.

We can't let the bastards get us down.

OCTOBER 2020

Out of the Closet and into the Streets

I celebrate Coming Out Day every October 11

Which is today. So, I thought a bit of history might be appreciated.

I was always gay but didn't know it. Then I refused to recognize it. Then I didn't admit it.

In 1973, I married a male accordion player (please judge). What was I thinking? About the marriage? I wasn't. About the accordion? I was instantly sorry. You haven't suffered until you've heard "Jerimiah Was a Bullfrog" on the accordion.

And while the musician played his night and weekend gigs, I began hanging out with theater friends, going to cast parties, shows, and DC gay bars. I had a blast with the gay guys, but oddly I didn't meet a single gay woman.

My ludicrous marriage lasted six interminable years. My own Lawrence Welk worked as a lawyer by day and musician by night. We didn't see each other too much, which was good. Life wasn't horrible. Finally, on my thirtieth birthday, in 1978, I flipped out. I couldn't take one more night in a hotel lobby waiting for his Bar Mitzvah gig to end. I fled.

My theater friends tried to help me figure out why (besides the accordion) I left my marriage. That's when my college roommate called and asked if I'd visit her in Cape Cod. And, intuitive gal she was, Lesley took me for a day in Provincetown.

I didn't know what hit me. Gay couples everywhere. We stopped at the Womencrafts bookshop, a small, crowded space bulging with lesbian literature, feminist gifts, and crafts. Too afraid to investigate any of the books, I absorbed everything that leapt into my path: buttons proclaiming, "The Moral Majority is

Neither" and "A Woman without a Man is like a Fish without a Bicycle;" posters, T-shirts and mugs celebrating feminism, pro-choice and other familiar topics.

Lesley paid for a stained-glass seagull while I stared at the short-haired, makeup-free women behind the cash register. Were they, you know? I picked up a mug with a photo of Robert Indiana's LOVE sculpture on it and took it to the register.

"That will be $4.99 after the 10 percent lesbian discount," said the clerk. Holy shit. My face flushed and I bobbled my wallet trying to get to my money to pay for my lesbian-discounted mug. Then I clutched my purchase and ran out to Commercial Street, sweat beading up on my forehead and knees weak with panic. Like an undercover cop in trouble, I'd been made.

And it hit me. I was a lesbian. It all made sense. Yes. Lesbian. Right there on Commercial Street I had an epiphany. I also had a lobster roll and kept looking around.

Dodging bikes and bodies on the teeming honky-tonk stretch, Lesley and I saw the incredible number of men, in couples, flowing with the tide. There were more men wearing earrings than women. On the other hand, a lot of the women resembled beefy men. I shamelessly gawked.

Then, a tough-looking woman wearing a "Don't Die Wondering" button side-stepped a scooter and ran smack into me. "Excuse me," she mumbled, using her muscular arms to fend me off as I stared at the words "Don't Die Wondering" under my nose. I turned to gape as she charged down the street and almost did die wondering as a crazed biker nearly took me out.

So, I went home, talked to myself about the theater actresses I'd had debilitating "crushes" on, the episodes of *Cagney & Lacey* I couldn't miss, and the ennui in my marital bed. Yeah, time to peek out of the closet.

I was terrified to tell friends and family I was gay. Paranoid and miserable, I loitered in the library, stealthily reading up on homosexuality. And back then, the news wasn't so good. It seemed I'd have to learn to play softball.

Fortunately, the *Washington Blade* newspaper gave me hope. The paper's headlines hawked liberal legislation, successful gay businesspeople, book and movie reviews, and a list of support organizations a mile long. I could join gay democrats, go gay roller skating, sing with a gay chorus, and even pray at a gay synagogue. What? To find a nice Jewish girl?

Damned if I didn't. After stealthy solo visits to seedy lesbian bars and trips to the DC Women's Center, plus some odd but informative one-off dates, I met a woman who became my first lover. Okay, I was out to me. And her, of course, but firmly in the closet elsewhere.

It took another year to meet Bonnie, the woman who has been my spouse for the last thirty-eight years. Back then I came out to my father ("Oh boy, I need a Scotch!"), my boss ("Um, that's nice. I don't care"—but he did), and the whole world in print in LGBTQ publications.

I moved to Rehoboth Beach, DE, or as I call it "Gayberry, RFD." And would flagrantly disobey that button seen in Provincetown in 1978. No, I would not die wondering. I'm queer, I'm here, I never had to play softball, and I never have to listen to "Lady of Spain" again.

NOVEMBER 2020

The Margin of Error

I'm sitting here at press time, nauseously optimistic, hoping that Joe Biden will be our next president. The presidency has not been decided yet, but Joe Biden has a razor thin lead—along with the promise of a cascade of lawsuits, and fully half the country hating the other half.

Is the margin of error my error? For the life of me I cannot understand how 50 percent of Americans still support Trump. I'm sad, angry, and baffled. As for the pollsters, "You're fired!" if you'll excuse the expression.

It's ironic that it was election eve 2016 when I was putting my book *Fried and Convicted* together. I was certain that the last essay would be written immediately after the election, congratulating Hillary and joyously heading into a new and exciting era.

Shit happens. And on that bleak morning after, none of us envisioned exactly how much shit would happen in the next almost-four years. Back then, knowing I could not end *Fried and Convicted* with an essay that had me figuratively slitting my wrists, I held the book back a couple of months to include a few lighter stories to soften the blow. But for those of us watching the dumpster fire that was the Trump administration, the blows did not stop.

Consequently, these last three years of essays were written with me trying to soften my gnashing of teeth. Oddly, when I turned off the news and stopped spitting, I did have some entertaining experiences and was able to write about other things. Enough, that my publishers felt I should eventually conclude the history of my LGBTQ political and social life in Rehoboth with one more "frying" book. So, I will.

Meanwhile, folks still ask "What's with the *frying* thing?" It was another margin of error. I named my 2004 collection *As I Lay Frying*, a super-silly literary pun from a 1996 essay I wrote as I lay on the Gordon's Pond beach, slathered in sunscreen and giddy to be amid hundreds of lesbians splayed on the sand. I was thrilled I'd be published and certain the book would be a local one-off flash in the pan with a funny name.

Writers plan and the universe laughs. While it was good to hear the laughter, it prompted somebody to say "You should name the next book *Fried & True*." Next book?

Well, I was still writing for *Letters*, with essays piling up, gay rights progress being made in Delaware, and activism lighting up our hometown. Over two wonderful decades, three more collections followed: *For Frying Out Loud, Time Fries,* and *Fried & Convicted*.

I'm proud to say that as a series, the books chart Rehoboth life through three Delaware governors, the rise of a Speaker of the House, and CAMP Rehoboth's brilliant success in becoming not just an LGBTQ community center, but truly the heart of the community. There were years of volunteer strategy sessions testimony, letter-writing, and hard-fought legislative success—from a simple anti-discrimination bill to civil unions, marriage equality, and transgender protections. It took the work of many and proved to be a truly thrilling and satisfying effort.

Will we now start the slide backward? Only time will tell.

But as I sit here nibbling my nails and praying for an election victory, I've decided something. The title of my final collection will be inspired by the Jersey Boys' hit *Big Girls Don't Cry*—although this big girl shed many a tear over the last almost-four years of the despicable Trump administration.

Big Girls Don't Fry will end my magical quarter century-plus as a writer for *Letters* and more here in Delaware for our LGBTQ community. I'm honored to have witnessed it all and participated in much. I'm not going to press just yet. If there is a

Biden victory and if Trump slithers away *(editor's note: "Oy!")*, I may want to comment on the Inauguration and perhaps the first years of the Biden administration.

But right now, I just heard Bonnie scream. The election's been called! Joe Biden will be our next US president. The relief I feel is overwhelming. This writer has no words except, "Thank you, Joe Biden." Whew! Go, Joe! Go, Delaware! Go CAMP Rehoboth! I love you all.

DECEMBER 2020

Bye Bye 2020. I Need a Drink.

As 2020 hurtles toward closure (thank goodness!) are you completely nuts yet? Have current events and Covid, the disaster twins of contemporary life overtaken your good sense? Are you still the same person you were on New Year's Day 2020?

I most certainly am not.

I came out of the closet yesterday (ha, ha, that was in 1978) having switched out summer for winter clothes and realized I've not worn any of them since last March.

Can you believe this year? I'm writing this a week and a half before the issue hits the streets or various digital devices. Chaos reigns, with current events moving so fast I have no idea if, when we publish, life will have anything at all in common with today, when I'm writing. My friends in Canada said they feel like they're living in the apartment above a meth lab.

We're dealing with Trump's big election lie, still more Covid, inauguration threats, and all manner of terror. Every morning I need two cups of coffee and a GasX before turning on the news.

Recently, when friends from our COVID bubble invited us to a vodka and gin tasting, it seemed an appropriate event for these terrible times. Ever the vodka snob, I love my Grey Goose for a martini. Second is the pricey Belvedere, with its stunning etched-glass bottle. Mostly, though, I make do with the less expensive brands for adulterating vodka with cranberry or tonic.

So, I went to this event happily looking forward to seeing friends and taking my mind off the cascade of October and November surprises in the news. I knew this drinking game would be fun, but I had little anticipation of good news from the tastings.

"Gin or vodka?" asked the hostess. "Vodka," I said, flashing back to my being super snockered on gin as a college freshman. Even now, fifty-four years later, a sniff of Gilby's and I'm back in the dorm with my head in a bucket.

So vodka it was, as the hostess placed before me nine tiny plastic cups, each numbered and containing a half-shot of vodka. First test: we swirled the cup to see if the vodka had legs, like red wine, though I'd never heard of leggy vodka. But the longer the vodka splashes stay above the vodka remaining below, the better it is said to be.

It appeared that some taste test cases slowly drooled down while others sank like a concrete ankle bracelet on a gangster's foot. None of the vodkas had great legs (though the host did), but the slightly pink-tinted sample dried on the side of the cup on the way up. Yuk.

We went on to judge taste, balance, and overall appeal. I did some gentle sipping for taste, feeling the liquid on the tip of my tongue, swishing it around like Listerine, then swallowing. Listerine might have been preferable to one of the tastes. Most of them tasted darned good to me.

The next round had me sipping to determine balance, but I didn't know what the heck that was. Uneducated about balance, I just did a bottom's up times nine.

Lastly, we judged appeal. After nine slugs of vodka twice, who am I to judge? I mean it wasn't a gay bar pour, but still, nine tiny cups made a healthy double martini.

Then, the samples were to be scored from 1 (unacceptable) to 20 (exquisite). Frankly, from the first tastes, I knew what I liked based on the Goldilocks Scale—too strong, too weak, and *juuuust* right. The worst could have passed for rocket fuel and the best cried out for immediate ice and pimento-stuffed olives.

Here's the upshot. The scary pink stuff was unacceptable.

My dearest Grey Goose ($47.95 for 1.75L) was only a middling choice, as was Belvedere ($51.99), designer bottle be damned. My second top honors went to Tito's at $32.27.

But my overall favorite was, drumroll, Costco's Kirkland—$12.99 for the same size jug. Seriously.

Back at home, back to the news, I grabbed a funnel and filled the gorgeous Belvedere bottle with Kirkland. It's going to take a lot of this stuff to get me through December and into 2021 or whenever the &#*% we know who the US President will be.

As for me, when 5 p.m. comes, I'm hitting Costco's finest. And whatever your cocktail of choice may be, from Diet Coke to hot saki, enjoy!

Farewell, 2020. You were a mess. Hoping for happy new year.

JANUARY 2021

January 6th, Specifically

What the hell? I'm sitting here watching thugs with Trump banners pillage through the Capitol building. People with AK-47s, gas masks, all manner of weapons, racist T-shirts, tactical gear, and even one goofball wearing a hat with horns on it and a fur vest. WTH?

As I sit glued to the television, I cannot believe I'm watching an insurrection in my own country. MAGA guerillas are storming the Capitol, calling out for Nancy Pelosi, breaking windows, and fighting with the police. It's disgusting. And I think Trump told them to do it. How is this even possible? This is even more disgusting than the last four years, than the lie being told that Trump won the election, than the uptick in discrimination. WTH??

Happy New Year?

I'm so stunned I can't think of anything else to write. I'm just staring at the carnage on the TV . . . pardon me, but I think I will let others write and write and write and talk and blab and opine about this. I think I'm gonna concentrate on pure survival and hoping to make people laugh. At least I hope I can.

FEBRUARY 2021

It's a Real %&^# Show

No, not the aftermath of the insurrection, although militia men did defecate on the floor of Congress. And the ex-prez is still repeating shit-faced lies. All those things are still a mess and look to be for some time.

But this tale is about my dog. And he's fine. Now.

But one night I noticed that my schnauzer Windsor appeared to need Preparation H. *Ewwww.* Okay, that's probably the most descriptive I'm getting.

We agreed that his, um, symptom, was not life-threatening, and calmly decided to wait until morning to see the vet. Ten seconds later we completely freaked out and rushed to the twenty-four-hour clinic.

After waiting in the car for an hour in the dead of night (Covid, you know), and authorizing every kind of test, including an ultrasound, we eventually learned that our poor boy had a large polyp in his colon, situated quite near the end of the trolley line. And, to remove it, he needed abdominal surgery at a specialized clinic. Of course, he did.

But before the surgeons there could perform the operation, Windsor would need (wait for it) . . . a colonoscopy.

Seriously????

"And if you think you despise drinking that prep stuff, dogs hate it more." said the vet tech. My imagination went wild. Number One, I saw myself squirting prep down his gullet with a water gun. Number two, I worried about a lot of Number Two.

But as fortune and our carpets would have it, Windsor was invited to the hospital and given twilight drugs so he could dream of Snausages while a nasal tube delivered the medication. Blessedly, what happened at the vet stayed at the vet. But it amused me that simultaneously both my dog and my bank account were totally cleaned out.

Once the docs had a pristine playing field, the patient was ready for his close-up, Mr. DeMille. The polyp was surgically removed, and a woozy Windsor was discharged wearing a massive plastic cone around his neck and head. A dog's instinct to lick his wounds is primordial. So, it was not *Get Smart's* cone of silence, as the dog made pathetic sounds trying to gnaw his way out of his head gear.

"Wait, I have an idea," my spouse said, turning into Walmart. She came back to the car with a size eighteen-month children's onesie outfit.

"It's got little dinosaurs on it," she said.

I could not picture how this was going to help.

Back home, we removed the cone of shame from Windsor's head, slipped the onesie suit on him, front paws through the sleeves, the shirt covering his back and belly, and snapping at his caboose. We fastened two of the four posterior snaps, leaving the center open for his stubby little tail to stick out. I have to say, it was adorable.

And I think he was so shocked to be wearing a dinosaur suit that for the entire two weeks after surgery, he pranced around like a supermodel on the runway and never once tried to investigate his belly wound. We even got the little fashionista additional outfits for his own personal Fashion Week.

When the vet called and asked us to email her a photo of his incision to make sure it didn't look infected, we complied. But I panicked. If I emailed a photo of my male dog's torso, was I sexting? I flashed back to the Anthony Weiner (unfortunate name) scandal and wondered if Windsor or I would get the jail time. And I kept checking my mail for valentines from girl Schnauzers.

Of course, the best news is that Windsor is well. But almost as great is the fact that we had a pet insurance policy. Heads up:

pet medical care is expensive – as it should be for the expert care they need and get.

But a pet insurance plan for a young dog or cat is relatively inexpensive–and get this, it paid 80 percent (less a $300 deductible) of the entire hit to my credit card, which, by the way, cost as much as a slightly used Buick. It was easy to file a claim and we got paid back very fast. My insurance company could take a lesson.

So, Windsor reports that his parents felt as much relief for having the insurance as he did for having lost a polyp. And face it, would a well-dressed sleeping dog lie?

APRIL 2021

It's Officially Poodle Beach!
The Definitive or Not so Definitive Word on Rehoboth's Gay Beach

Poodle Beach off the Rehoboth Beach boardwalk is the previously unofficial, but now historically official name for Rehoboth's beachfront from Queen and Prospect streets to the south end of the boardwalk. It's where the boys are, and none too few gals as well.

Every year, or occasionally every other year, there are articles about why that stretch is called Poodle Beach. Rehoboth residents and regulars don't mind reading about it seasonally, and newcomers get the real, or partially real, scoop about why that sandy oasis is called Poodle Beach.

Sort of. Because frankly, nobody really knows.

Historians have long tapped Carpenter Beach, just over the dunes and heading towards south, as Rehoboth's first gay beach.

That sandy stretch was the home of Louisa Dupont Carpenter, an aviatrix and—though married to a man—known to enjoy the lesbian lifestyle. One of her closest friends was Hollywood legend Tallulah Bankhead, who often visited Louisa there, along with many homosexual male friends, during the 1930s and '40s. Louisa's gal pal was torch singer Libby Holman, who, when accused of shooting her husband, tobacco heir Zachery Smith Reynolds, was bailed from jail by Louisa. Libby and Louisa took refuge from the scandal (the charges were eventually dropped) and came to live here in the mansion on Carpenter Beach (it's a great story, look it up!).

So Carpenter Beach became a known gathering spot for gay visitors and continued that way through the '50s, '60s and early '70s. Hundreds of older gay men would sun and socialize there, playing chess, backgammon, and volleyball a comfortable distance away from the vacationing straight couples and families on the official Rehoboth beach.

Gay people faced the awful threat of exposure, firings, and even prison back then, so staying to themselves at Carpenter Beach made sense.

According to reports from those who were there, it was a very sophisticated gay scene, and the tradition went on for years. As there were no gay bars in Rehoboth in those days (and even if there were, it was against the law to walk with a drink in your hand, so nobody could socialize), gay visitors spent time on Carpenter Beach followed by private house parties—with shades drawn and discretion a must.

The tradition continued almost unchanged through the 1960s and early '70s. Louisa du Pont Carpenter was still around at her beach home much of the time but died in the mid-'70s after she crashed her single-engine plane trying to land at an eastern shore airport.

Why, then, don't we still plant our rainbow flags there?

In the late '70s or early '80s, even with the threat of being outed, old-timers recall two men who may or may not have been "cousins," who got fed up dragging their beach chairs and coolers all that way past the boardwalk. And they longed to be closer to boardwalk refreshments as well.

One day, they brazenly spread their blankets on the sand near Queen Street, and invited friends to join them. Soon, this growing collection of gays took a stand on the sand, holding their ground as the Rehoboth family crowd moved slightly north to accommodate them.

For a few years after that, a group of old-timers still frequented Carpenter Beach, with their chess and backgammon games but eventually the shift to Queen Street became permanent, and Poodle Beach was born.

But wait! Why did this "new" area become known as Poodle Beach? Perhaps, it was a hurled slur, or maybe those "cousins" had poodles. Some recall that they did indeed have fluffy white (or were they black?) standard poodles with them. The truth is the naming of the beach remains a mystery.

And into the new millennium, Poodle Beach became more and more famous, crowded, home to legendary Drag Volleyball, and iconic to Rehoboth Beach. So iconic, in fact, that resident Frank Cooper, along with his friends, had been trying to find a way to commemorate the history of Poodle Beach.

Cooper petitioned the state of Delaware for a historical marker to acknowledge Poodle Beach as a historic refuge for LGBTQ people to have fun and relaxation, away from discrimination and harassment for over seventy years.

The Delaware Public Archives Historical Marker Program approved the marker, one of over 600 in the state, in December 2020. Wording on the sign and placement of the marker are still in the works.

The name and its relation to poodles may remain a mystery but its popularity surely is not. And as of now, Poodle Beach is here, it's queer, and it's recognized as historic.

JUNE 2021

First Plague, then Pestilence?

June is busting out all over. And I'm terrified.

The East Coast is expected to be a hot spot for Brood X, the seventeen-year cicadas. Frankly, having this happen now makes sense. We've had the plague and now we get pestilence.

And as I write, the Great Eastern Brood, as they are also called, is prepping to claw their way up from their long underground slumber and infest the mid-Atlantic by the billions for two or three hideous weeks.

Entomologists seem to worship these creatures. I find them a disgusting, annoying, invading bug battalion. Cicadas emerge as immature nymphs from underground locations where they've been drinking craft-brewed tree sap all their lives. As soon as they leave home, these baby bugs molt into adult cicadas with five eerie red eyes, an exoskeleton, and wings.

Ugh. And they act like college freshmen. Cicadas sing Kumbaya by making high-pitched sounds from flapping their tymbals, a membrane on their bellies. Each cicada can make as much noise as a single lawnmower. With 1.5 million of them performing per acre, it's a regular seventeen-year Woodstock, making a neighbor with a leaf blower sound like a lullaby.

And these freshmen binge drink to excess in their tree-stump dorms, sucking up water meant for our gardens.

And, holy cow, do they have sex. As soon as they mate, the females land on tree trunks and branches, split the bark, and lay eggs—up to 600 eggs in their lifetime. It's a cicada baby boom.

Having been educated that these annoying pests do not bite, sting, or release venom doesn't keep me from despising them. My first Brood X barrage was in 1970 in Bethesda, MD. I was a recent college grad in my tie-dyed shirt, hippie bell bottoms, and

Birkenstocks. It was freaky, man. Outside my psychedelically decorated apartment cicadas strafed our window screens and made such a din we had to read lips to watch *Marcus Welby M.D.* and *The Mod Squad.*

Groovy but disgusting, I walked on sidewalks five bodies deep in dead cicadas. I had to rethink my choice of footwear. Ugh.

It was 1984 when we met again, on a gorgeous spring afternoon as I drove to a Baltimore Oriole's game at the old Memorial Stadium. As I sped down Thirty-Third Street in my new Mustang convertible, I was besieged by a wall of golf-ball-sized flying insects headed for my head. Incoming! I couldn't see, so I ducked below the windshield and pulled over to the curb to endure hand-to-hand combat with the enemy.

I got the convertible top up but dammit, I'd taken prisoners. It took me fifteen minutes making like *The Karate Kid* to get the vile creatures out of my car and me back on the road. Not at all my idea of getting buzzed.

2004 wasn't bad. I'd moved to Rehoboth in a neighborhood where everything was brand-new construction, and the underground cicada lairs must have been destroyed. I saw very few near my house, which suited me just fine. Visiting in Maryland, I could hear them in the trees, and I got dive-bombed a bit and my dog Moxie got a belly-ache from over-snacking on the bodies on the ground.

Apparently, humans were snacking on them too, as reality cooking shows offered gourmet cicada recipes and critics touted Brood X deliciousness. Yuk.

For 2021 will we be lucky? News articles warn of a Brood X bumper crop just waiting to buzz us, deafen us, and be crunched underfoot.

Great, outdoor dining will be impossible just as Covid makes us need it most. And good thing my current schnauzer knows better than to eat anything not delivered from Chewy.

com. As for me, I still won't cave to gourmet cicada recipes, but I guess I will crankily put up with the infestation.

And hey, seventeen years from now when Brood X returns in 2038, if I'm lucky enough to still be here, I'll be 90. I hope I'm pretty deaf and not tempted by cicada tastings. But I'll welcome the brood home and be happy to see them.

After all, together, we've come a long way, baby bugs.

JUNE 2021

No Police in Parade? Shame!

A news article at the end of May punched me in the gut and sent me flying to the computer to speak out.

Police Banned from Participating in New York City Pride Events until 2025

What?

According to news reports, the governing body for the New York Pride Parade has banned police participation because "The sense of safety that law enforcement is meant to provide can instead be threatening, and at times dangerous, to those in our community who are most often targeted with excessive force and/or without reason."

Look, we all know, and have seen, video of very bad apples among law enforcement. And yes, we are in an era where Black lives certainly matter, transgender lives need the support of us all, and many other issues can cast a bad light on some law enforcement officers and departments.

But good God, let's not throw out the baby with the dirty bathwater.

I remember years of attendance at the very New York City Pride Parade that now bans police from marching. I remember the thrill I felt years ago seeing the Police Marching Band participating for the first time.

I remember 2013 and the bank of gay police officers gleefully accompanying Parade Marshall Edie Windsor the year she won her marriage equality case in the Supreme Court.

One year I found myself standing beside club legend Rollerena, who began skating on Christopher Street in the 1970s and who was now a senior drag queen still on roller skates. She was having trouble negotiating the busy street when a police officer politely asked some marchers make room for her, so she would not get hurt.

I remember New York's massive Fiftieth Anniversary of Stonewall Parade, which turned into a gigantic international pride celebration, flooding the streets of lower Manhattan with literally millions of people and tons of rainbow gear. And I saw the thousands of police officers keeping the peace and helping clear the intersections as the deluge of people traversed the crowded streets and sidewalks. I loved seeing some of the officers cheering us on, smiling, waving, enjoying their responsibility to keep us all safe.

There was no them and us. I saw no incidents of disrespect. There might have been some incidents in a crowd that large, but we read no reports of trouble.

But closer to home, twenty-five to thirty years ago in Rehoboth things were strained between the police and gay community. That's when the late Steve Elkins and the fledgling CAMP Rehoboth organization met with Rehoboth Police to forge new era of cooperation in fighting boardwalk gay bashings and discrimination.

After a particularly horrid incident of gay bashing, the police department and CAMP Rehoboth got together for what was then called "sensitivity training" for their officers. It was a job that started as a chore for both CAMP staff and the officers. It turned into a warm, friendly session of ideas exchanged and friends made.

Following came years and years of Rehoboth police officers congenially standing guard at big dances, events and auctions at the Convention Center, at the CAMP block parties and being responsive to every single call or communication from CAMP Rehoboth.

There was a bridging of the cultural gap between the LGBTQ community and the police. And the straight community. And the other nonprofits. And the business community. The list goes on.

And I certainly cannot forget the police officers in full uniform, the police department flag at half mast, and officers openly grieving at the 2018 memorial service for the late CAMP Rehoboth Executive Director Steve Elkins.

Heaven help us if we echo the misguided decision by the New York Pride organization to break the terrific bonds we have nurtured with our local law enforcement.

Shame, shame.

AUGUST 2021

Let's Get Physical

It's August already and I'm aging more gracelessly than usual. But at least I'm vaccinated, out and about, trying to remember what life used to be like.

The fact that I lost more than a year of touring with my one-woman show, *Aging Gracelessly: 50 Shades of Fay*, is significant.

I mean hell, I broke into show business at an age I'd more likely break a hip, so a lost year is big. How big? This morning on Facebook somebody posted "Life is like a roll of toilet paper. The closer you get to the end, the faster it goes."

Tell me about it. We're deteriorating at a rapid rate. My wife recently had a knee replacement made necessary by an injury she got putting out the garbage. And I suffered a torn rotator cuff in my shoulder tripping over that same garbage before it went out. We've both spent the past few months at physical therapy.

This is where we see our friends now. Physical therapy. We used to meet at protest rallies, dance clubs, and bars. Now we're grunting side by side on adjoining gurneys. Hell, we used to smoke joints, not replace them.

Our grandparents did not go to physical therapy. Something hurt, they sat down. They stayed home, eating hard candy from a silver candy dish and watching Lawrence Welk. *We* go to physical therapy.

My wife comes home from therapy, and I ask, "Who'd you see today?" "Everybody!" she says. It's half the golf league and three-quarters of the pickleball team.

I know we boomers trend younger and stay more active than our parents did, but it has consequences—like having to be someplace every Tuesday and Thursday morning. We practice things like sitting down and getting up. We stretch enormous rubber bands that could, if mishandled, can take your eye out. We sit under huge icepacks while little electronic muscle stimulators give us the full taser experience.

When I started shoulder therapy, they asked me my goal for recovery. My goal is to make the pain stop. That's it. Since there's no more Ringling Brothers Circus, I'm not considering a career as a trapeze artist. I don't need full function back. I just want to be pain-free lifting a Cosmo to my mouth.

One exercise has me lying on my back and trying to lift a golf club over my head. I realize this is the closest I'll ever get to pumping iron. And no, I cannot lift the damn thing all the way up. But halfway gets me to Cosmo territory.

One of my pals says her doctor prescribed medical marijuana for her shoulder pain. I asked if it helped. She told me the pain is as bad as ever, but now she doesn't give a damn. I liked the sound of that.

We even try to fix our brains. I know you've seen those TV ads for Prevagen. I was thinking about starting on it until I found out it costs $79 a bottle. I figured I didn't need it since I remembered that $79 is a lot of money.

Although conversations with my friends are starting to sound eerily similar. "You know, what's-her-name, right? We met at the fish place, um, whatchamacallit."

Well, the good news is that in June the CDC gave us the green light to open things up and I'm back on the show biz circuit again. Bookings are coming in, and my career as the last comic sitting is back on track. My wife is teeing up on the golf course again, and my shoulder feels a whole lot better.

I'll be up moving, telling stories, and at happy hours ordering top shelf cocktails even if I am no longer capable of reaching the top shelf.

OCTOBER 2021

Curtain Up, Light the Lights, Cue the Schnauzer

I'm so happy the pandemic seems to be waning so I can be back on the road as the last comic sitting.

To my delighted surprise, my one-woman show, *Aging Gracelessly: 50 Shades of Fay* is still getting bookings. I'm thrilled to be on stage at my age. Hell, at any age.

You see, back in the day, I was a college theater major. In my first starring role, just as I stepped out of the wings onto stage, someone behind me said, "My God, you can see right through her dress." There's a confidence builder.

But my budding performing career came to a screeching halt the next morning with a review in the old *Washington Star* newspaper. The critic said I played Madame Arkadina in Chekhov's *The Seagull* like Zasu Pitts. You may not recall that fluttery, fussy 1950s actress, but the comparison was not a compliment. I made my early career as a director instead.

But a funny thing happened on my way to old age. When reading my columns aloud at writers' conferences, listeners laughed. Expecting smiles, I got guffaws.

And in turn, my writer colleagues, most of them reading deadly serious fiction or truly tragic memoirs, positively refused to read following me. So, I was always relegated to last reader on the panel, often missing happy hour entirely, But a lot of people told me I should do stand-up comedy. Seriously?

Well, only a mere half century after my early critical humiliation, I began thinking about getting back on stage. This time, instead of Chekhov, I'd perform my published columns, including almost twenty years of flotsam and jetsam on these pages.

I started by reading my stories at a local bar. While I could enjoy a Cosmo instantly after finishing up, the audience was often a couple of martinis ahead of me, making their laughter raucous but their attention span spotty. I was Mrs. Maisel getting heckled long before there was a Mrs. Maisel. But it was fun.

My first real show was in 2015. I cobbled my humor stories together with a narrative about life with my mate Bonnie and a succession of miniature schnauzers—including tales of early closeted life, marching for our rights, moving to Rehoboth, and finding my voice in print. Not to mention stories of getting skunk sprayed, dangling from a zip line, living on a boat in Dewey, and aging quite gracelessly.

As I was now far too old to memorize the material, I performed seated on a stool, reading from a script on a music stand. The press release coined the phrase "sit-down comic." If it's good enough for David Sedaris to sit and read on stage, I would follow his lead.

Over the last eight years I've done the show more than sixty times, in theaters, clubs, churches, community centers, and on one enormous cruise ship. I had to clutch my bouncing script and hang onto my seat as the ocean liner lurched from side to side. The audience was rolling in the aisles but not necessarily from the jokes.

When I stood up for the curtain call, I couldn't tell if the audience was standing to cheer or abandon ship. I've played to crowds of more than 200 people and, at an underpublicized gig, to four inebriated drag queens and my entourage of six friends. I played outdoors in 100-degree heat and literally had heat stroke by the curtain call, as well as at New York's famed Duplex Cabaret where I was humbled to be on the same stage that spotlighted Barbra Streisand and Joan Rivers.

My troupe includes Bonnie handling sound cues and my schnauzer windsor sometimes coming on stage for the curtain call.

I've done makeup in dressing rooms with Hollywood mirrors

and in restaurant kitchen alcoves smelling like sausage and lit by a single dim bulb. I was the dim bulb for booking that one.

Accommodations have included living room futons, sketchy motels, luxury hotels, and a historic mansion with allergy-inducing mold from the gilded age. That night I sounded like the Lewes Ferry foghorn.

I just returned from shows in Ontario and Vermont, and this month I'm booked for a vegan, fragrance-free, back-to-nature women's weekend in the woods. I think they've reserved me a yurt. I'm praying for a flush toilet.

Yes, I'm having a grand time and hope to stay in show biz as long as I can. I just heard from a very dear mentor who, at 85, for her assisted living facility talent shows enters on her scooter noting she's a stand-up comic who can't stand up. Way to go. If I must, I'll follow in her tire tracks.

After all, I'm careful not to wear transparent costumes, and the old *Washington Star* folded in 1981.

Curtain up.

APRIL 2022

It's How I Roll

I ride a monster trike, a massive, thundering, fire-breathing three-wheeler. I am fierce.

Kidding. It's no Harley. In fact, I'm the only one I know who's ever fallen off an adult tricycle. Not that the accident was my fault. I was traveling quite robustly when the chain snapped, sending me into a curb, tipping the vehicle, and tossing my butt into the gutter.

Luckily, my wife was the only witness.

After ensuring I wasn't hurt, but fearing I'd never get on the $600 beast again, she babbled, "It's not your fault! The chain broke! You did good!" Please, the toddler down the block could have held on.

Truth is, I've never been a biker. You don't ride bikes in Manhattan unless you're a courier with a death wish.

Once, almost forty years ago, trying to impress the athletic person who became my spouse anyway, I bought my first bicycle. I recruited friends to push me off and run after me yelling "You can do it!!!"

Then, just days later I showed up to bike twenty-five miles on Maryland's Eastern Shore. Fortunately, the whole route, like Delaware, was totally flat terrain. Off we went, and I made chipper conversation to mask my panicked wobbling. We completed the schlep and followed up with cocktails. Not to mention Preparation H.

Then, of all horrors, Bonnie thought I was a true biking enthusiast and planned a Nantucket cycling weekend. Okay, I admit to feeling smugly superior when others sat in cars on the ferry and I stood with my bike, backpack, and a tiny rear-view mirror clipped to my sunglasses.

But then we docked. The streets were cobblestone and could shake loose a kidney. And two bumpy blocks later came a humongous paved hill, straight up like a Swiss alp to our hotel, the Lucretia Mott House.

Lucretia, it turns out, was a hardy nineteenth-century feminist, civil rights activist, and organizer of the very first Women's Rights Conference at Seneca Falls, New York. I bet she biked there from Boston. I'm not as hardy as Lucretia, who probably carried a bike on her head up the hill to her house every day. I could barely drag the thing up.

Instead of planting a flag at the summit I planted my bike at the first tavern – and toasted to my lucky break with the weather. It rained for two days, leaving us biking little and bar-hopping much. Bye Lucretia.

When we got home, having been spared the Tour de Nantucket, I hung the two-wheeler on hooks in the garage where it rusted to the wall and conveyed with the house.

So, four decades later, I picked up my old-lady trike from the street and walked it to the bike shop. It will live to ride another day.

In fact, this morning my wife biked alongside me as I brazenly tricycled along an official bike path to a lunchtime rendezvous with friends. I was passed by speeding cyclists clad in moisture-wicking bike outfits while I schvitzed into a ratty Rehoboth T-shirt. We were joined by a remarkable number of people pushing baby strollers and chauffeuring aging Chihuahuas and Shih Tzus.

I pedaled along, quickly coming to a bridge advertising a ten-ton limit. Despite last night's loaded nachos, I was pretty sure I was okay. But just around the next curve, a fat buzzard with beady eyes swooped to a landing in front of me. This turkey vulture watched me struggling to pedal and envisioned roadkill.

I denied him brunch and kept on. At one point, this chicken had to cross the road to get to the other side. I did fine stopping traffic in the crosswalk, but then encountered a steep sidewalk and started to roll backward towards the street. "Pedal faster!" screamed a passenger in a car stopped still for fear I'd roll back in front of him momentarily.

I made it. I met our friends for lunch. We ordered Pain Killer cocktails in honor of my backside, and I steeled myself for the eventual trek home.

"That's a snazzy trike," one of my friends said. "Can I try it out and ride it back to your house? You can ride in the car with my husband."

Some days are just lucky like that.

And by the way. I've named my trike Lucretia Mott. She's hardy. And quite the activist for getting me pedaling. Let the good times roll.

MAY 2022

The Game of Crones

As a rule, I don't participate in anything where there are ambulances standing by (think polar bear plunge) or waivers to sign. That would be for axe-throwing and the latest world-wide craze for axe-throwing bars.

Axes and alcohol. What could go wrong?

Apparently nothing as this axe bar trend is sweeping the country without incident.

I read of bars called hatchet hangouts hosting bachelorette parties, middle school birthdays, axe leagues, and all matter of hipsters throwing weapons just for fun.

The craze started in 2011, when an axe-throwing bar opened in Toronto. Since then, axe bars are thriving all over Canada and the US, attracting stressed-out millennials drinking and launching axes.

Researching, I learned that hatchets and axes were born of medieval battle-axe weapons. Oh boy. It also brought to mind numerous cartoonists and mid-twentieth-century comedy writers describing nagging wives, mothers-in-law, or people like Nurse Ratched as battle-axes.

I was right, as directly under that Wiki entry came another: *Battle-Axe: a formidable woman, aggressive, domineering and forceful.* And the definition was accompanied by a picture of militant temperance activist Carrie Nation brandishing a hatchet. Yikes.

Even weirder, I slid down the rabbit hole to a discussion of older lesbian women reclaiming the word crone and defining it as the age when they are wise and powerful. And their symbol is . . . wait for it—a silver battle-axe! Hmmm, have I found my people?

But I admit, researching axe-throwing worried me. What if my digital fingerprints caused police attention if an axe murderer was on the loose? ("Columnist researched axe throwing prior to gruesome crime.")

Also, on the rare occasion when I go bowling, I've been known to have fingers securely implanted in my bowling ball and still shoot the ball backward towards screaming people. If I took up axe-throwing could the axe boomerang?

Qualms aside and sorely needing a topic for this upcoming deadline, I looked up our local axe bar. While editorial rules frown on my mentioning this great venue's name, I can say that patrons have the choice of throwing axes as righties or Lefty's. And it was at this venue, in the name of crones everywhere, I vowed to check out axe-throwing bars.

Of course, things sporty and alcoholic are always best with a group, so I enlisted several other senior citizen friends for this potentially risky business.

After ordering yummy appetizers and beer (sorry, Carrie Nation), we met our instructor. He sported the requisite full beard, flannel shirt, and cowboy pants. Paul Bunyan was a thoroughly delightful person, and I suspect, out of uniform, he'd no longer look like an extra from *Deliverance*.

The sport appeared simple. Send an axe flying to embed itself into the eight-foot-wide wooden wall with the enormous bull's-eye on it.

Our *axepert* showed us proper technique and stressed the safety rules. He coached us to hold the axe over our heads, one or two handed, draw back and let it fly.

Despite copying his form and picturing a car warranty robo-spammer as my target, my weapon wobbled in the air, hit the wall sideways, and flopped to the floor. Safety rules prevented me from retrieving it. That was good since my spouse took a turn and made a quick, deeply embedded bull's-eye. I shuddered. I did not ask who she pictured as the target.

Two more members of team geezer took turns, alternately throwing their axes on the floor below the target and hollering about their rotator cuffs. Ultimately, both got the hang of it and made several impressive bull's-eyes. There was much laughter during this game of crones as we defiantly toasted to Carrie Nation.

As it turned out, all of us succeeded in burying the hatchet in the wall, if not the bull's-eye, at least once. It was fun and nobody went home in a sling. Or worse.

I think I like my new hobby. As long as nobody calls me an old battle-axe. I will, however, willingly answer to crone.

MAY 2022

Grocery Store Hunger Games

In my late teens I applied for a summer job bagging groceries. But while waiting for a call, I got a gig as a summer camp drama counselor. That job launched my theater career but left my resume without cash register or grocery-bagging experience.

It's not too late! A half century later there's the fresh hell of grocery store self-checkout. I hate it.

Yesterday, the scanner refused to ring up a buy-one-get-one deal and I had to drop everything to hunt down a human. The shopper waiting behind me got mad when I left my duty station, and it seemed like a lot of chaos for an English muffin BOGO.

And there's so little space on the kiosk counter I'm forever dropping things. A rolling stone may not gather moss, but a rolling avocado does. And this old bagger has no idea how to bag cans and bottles so you can pick it up without a forklift.

Oh, but my favorite is the busybody at the Walmart exit wanting to study my receipt. Puleeze. If you're going to make me to scan my stuff, don't treat me like a shoplifter on the way out. I have no intention of going to jail over a Vidalia onion.

And at this point I'm more of an employee than a customer anyway. I bought lunch at a Walmart the other day and felt perfectly entitled to eat it in the break room.

But apparently people do steal. Stores call shoplifting "external shrinkage," which is corporate speak for mega-theft. One scheme is weight abuse (not just from buying Oreos) from weighing cheap green beans while stacking a pricey bag of smoked salmon on top.

Then there's the banana maneuver, where shoppers peel codes off banana peels and put them on expensive steaks. Then, the stores hire more security folks as they lay off human cashiers.

It's all bananas.

But here's the thing. Some young people tell me they prefer no human contact. No waiting, no small talk, no help scanning or bagging. It's certain grocery cashiers are destined to go the way of bowling pin setters and town criers.

And restaurant waitstaff better watch their backs. I don't mind a QR code on the table to pull up a menu on my phone. I'm quite giddy, actually, having figured out how to do it. But I was just someplace where I had to place my entire dinner order on my phone—and it wasn't simple. See the four people, heads down, fooling with their phones instead of chatting and laughing like we planned.

The most confusing part was the request for a tip amount when the order was placed. On what do I base this? Do I tip myself for taking the order? To that point we'd seen only the hostess. Would our food be delivered by a Roomba?

All restaurants now have some form of digital service. What's with that digital bill where a server has you punch in a tip? Have you noticed, reading left to right, the first suggested tip is 30 percent. It's Tipflation. I refuse to feel guilty scrolling over to 20 percent. Likewise, I'm getting over the Jewish guilt from pressing "no tip" for somebody who just hands me a bagel.

This loss of human contact is creeping into my own house. Yesterday, Alexa reminded me to go to the back yard to pick up dog poop. I'm fairly certain Bonnie and Alexa collaborated on that reminder. But two can play this game. This morning I had Alexa remind Bonnie to take her blood pressure meds. It's liberating to offload my nagging. Although I forgot about Alexa when we went away and had a renter in our house. On his first morning there, he nearly stroked out when Alexa told him pick up dog poop. He didn't even have a dog.

Yes, I fear we are heading to a humanless hell. Although, dinosaurs are back on screen these days and I cling to the hope that what goes around, comes around again. I'm off to see my favorite bartender now. Live and in person. Cheers for bluecheese olives and human mixologist contact.

MAY 2022

Make Sure Your Bladder Is Full, Said Nobody Ever

You'd think I was going to scale Mount Kilimanjaro.

I'm not. But if I was, I've got the tools. As I write we're prepping for a trip to Utah and five National Parks—with friends in a convoy of two RVs. The trip was purchased in 2019, canceled by Covid in 2020, out of the question in 2021, and now back on the calendar.

We're more than three years older than when we first signed up and wondering if we still have the stamina for the hiking and room in the duffel for the medications, CPAP machine and hearing aid chargers.

We're flying out to Salt Lake City, picking up the rental RVs, and heading to Canyonlands, Arches, Capital Reef, Bryce and Zion. And we are ready.

First, we bought hiking shoes. My spouse has made me wear them around the house for the last week to "break them in." I have a mountain in my kitchen, but it's only dirty dishes. I feel silly. But tromp around in hikers I do, preparing for the red rock outward bound.

While ordering the shoes I read about their purpose: to cushion and support human feet from abrasions from rough wilderness, water, mud, or wildlife underfoot. I almost canceled the trip right then and there. Face it, other travelers or bears will not find themselves underfoot. I know what they meant. *Noooooo!*

As for wilderness, there's guaranteed to be thousands of other tourists tromping along these same trails we are, so wilderness is probably a thing of the past. It's possible it will be so populated we'll be wise to mask up.

We also bought hiking sticks (to beat back the wildlife?)

and backpacks with water bladders. I figure that the Amazon delivery guy thinks new people bought our house.

So where should we try out the hiking sticks? The only two-degree rise in Delaware is the one on my treadmill. I'd look pretty silly using my trekking poles to walk into Wawa. The poles collapse down for easy packing. Better them than me.

We decided we didn't need the anti-shock poles, which have an extra spring in them to absorb the shock of walking for people with unstable knees, hips, and ankles. Heck, that's me but unless it was going to absorb the shock of going on this trip at all, I went for saving money.

Our vacation partners called this morning and told me they cleaned out their bladders yesterday. This gave me pause. I clean out my bladder several times during the night but that's apparently not what they meant.

Oh, the bladders in the backpack. I guess it does make sense to clean out something you are ostensibly going to suck tepid water from while schlepping up trails and down canyons. So, I washed my backpack bladder, then tried on the backpack. I fought the urge to yodel like Heidi going up to feed sheep in the Alps.

Cleaning out my personal bladder figured into our rental requirements for the RV. The bed needed exits on both sides. We're too old to climb over one another, especially when nature is calling. That nature called for me to visit Utah's slotted canyons and grand rock arches and I agreed is still baffling to me.

Luckily, being equipped for RV travel is no problem as we're experienced. We know all about full hook-ups, where you get sewer, water, electric and sometimes even Wi-Fi and cable. We bring bug spray. As you might guess, I refuse to sleep any place with turf between me and a bathroom, so tent camping was out. The RV has carpeting on that path so I'm good.

Consulting a list of what to bring for day-hiking, I recognized some hikers' need for things like a compass, knife, flashlight and first aid kit, especially those hiking a long way to Tipperary. But I figure that at any point we're not going to be more than a mile from the visitor's center and a regulation toilet. After all, I am still me. And besides, I'm more worried about extra battery power for my iPhone camera, and perhaps a very loud whistle.

Oh, and in addition to hiking, some of us are going ziplining (been there, done that, barely survived, you probably read about it), rappelling into slot canyons (maybe), and a boat ride (for sure). Can't wait.

We do have to put together a shopping list for our campfire dinners (s'mores!) and food for lunch to take with us in the aforementioned backpacks. Nothing with mayonnaise, I guess.

While researching I found out that you can purchase a FEMA-approved one-week survival kit of nonperishable food that is disaster-proof and can be stored and safe for 25 years. I'm going with peanut butter and jelly instead. Although I liked the idea of disaster-proof.

Let's hope that this whole upcoming folly is disaster-proof. And there's a nightlight in the bathroom in the camper for cleaning out my bladders(s).

JUNE 2022

Postcards from the Edge of the Canyon

I just got back from Utah. First, without any snark whatsoever, let me say that the five National Parks in Utah (Canyonlands, Arches, Capital Reef, Bryce and Zion) are the most amazing and thrilling rural sights this New Yorker has ever seen.

They are hauntingly beautiful, each different, with towering rock formations and plunging canyons, massive vistas without any evidence of the twenty-first century, and the sound of silence so loud you could record it. Everything was breathtaking. Literally.

With park elevations from 4,000 to 8,500 feet above sea level, my breathing ranged from merely difficult to seeing stars and nearly passing out. Our Rehoboth house is seven feet above sea level and the highest I climb is onto a barstool at Aqua. What made me think I could do this?

But I did, schlepping up, across, and down many mountain trails, alternately gasping for air and taking selfies, most with my mouth agape desperately seeking oxygen.

With my trusty hiking shoes, trekking poles, and backpack's bladder filled with water to suck through a straw, I don't know if I was a poster girl for aging gracelessly or dead woman walking. We hiked to Mesa Arch at Canyonlands because the guidebook called it a "short, enjoyable, fairly level hike." Liars! It was my qualifying round for a knee replacement.

We loved driving on the canyon trails. Between drought conditions and high winds, it was a dustbowl drive, with actual sagebrush and tumbleweed rolling across the roads. We drove through a reddish haze of dust and sand, through tiny towns, places resembling the Bundy Compound or the Unabomber's house, grazing cows, buffalo, and circling buzzards. I prayed we wouldn't break down.

Finding provisions at the one Walmart within 200 miles was easy, but happy hour fixin's proved elusive. At a gas station we asked where to find a liquor store. Nobody knew. Overhearing our question, a wizened geezer said, "I think they sell some whiskey over there," pointing to the ramshackle restaurant next door. Turns out we'd stumbled upon State Liquor Store 42 in Green River, Utah.

There, in a small corner, amid Utah T-shirts and baseball caps, were several bottles, behind locked glass – one brand each of scotch, bourbon, vodka, gin and white wine.

My friend said, "See if they have a Sauvignon Blanc from New Zealand."

Puleeze, she got random yellow swill. It was not from New Zealand. The scotch would have been better as a charcoal starter.

About the RV. Readers might recall we had our own at one time and gleefully traveled all over. Um, we were younger then. Besides, this rental, unlike ours, had a bed with access only from the bottom. I longed for bathtub grab bars. Easiest for me was flopping onto my stomach and propelling myself with my elbows, like an infantryman crawling through the woods on his belly. The bed was pretty comfy, but getting back out at night to go to the bathroom required ninja warriorhood.

On a similar topic, while we hiked and climbed a lot, my most strenuous climb was back up into a Jeep 4x4. The damn thing was parked on a slope, and I had to hoist myself up and in. This embarrassing episode required the assistance of others and a goose from my wife.

On a wild ATV ride to the slot canyons, the wind picked up. Unfortunately, I was saying "Wow" about the scenery just as a sandstorm hit. From the sand in my teeth, I could have replenished the Jersey Shore.

Space precludes my telling you all the fantastic sights we saw and the fun we had. The scenery was stunning, and riding up to canyon rims (fortunately with professional guides driving), there were moments we felt like Thelma and Louise about to take the leap.

We took a boat ride on the Colorado River, hiked the winding trails, stared at the rock formations above and below, went off the grid for hours at a time (what? No service???) and had a blast. We laughed, we persevered, we ate a lot of hot dogs.

It was a fantastic and thrilling trip. Also, brutal. I loved the things I saw and did. But I'm glad to be home. My whole body hurts. It may be time for me to start acting my age.

FOR SALE
Hiking Boots
Trekking Sticks
Backpack with water bladder
Used once by a little old lady

Just kidding. I think.

NOVEMBER 2022

Sex, Lies and Video Hate

I went to the most marvelous party—as gay songwriter Noel Coward once sang. It was the wedding of two dear men, one of whom was responsible for writing Delaware's marriage equality law.

The moving ceremony was officiated by Delaware's first transgender state senator, who handled the task with authority, love, and humor.

It was a joyous night, with a beautiful diversity of guests, all ages, genders, ethnicities, and sexual orientations. It was a lovefest and a blast.

And I proved I'm clearly old, as I never even considered going to the after-party. My after-party was at Club Duvet. Z-z-z-z-z.

I went to sleep with a smile on my face and woke up to the horror of the Club Q murders.

I watched the story unfold, crying into my coffee, not understanding how this could happen again. I realized, beyond the gun culture and lack of mental health services, the true problem is the demonizing of minorities...

I've been alive long enough to have heard my grandparents and parents talking about the Holocaust. At the time, it was only a decade past a current event. My father fought against the Germans; my mother and her sister talked about the gas chambers in Yiddish, not to "frighten the kids."

But I learned about it all, including devouring books, films, and plays about the gassing of eight million Jews, gays, Romas (gypsies), people with disabilities and more. How could such a massive, inconceivable tragedy happen? We know the answer. It was facilitated by Hitler and the Nazis demonizing minority groups, fomenting hatred, and turning neighbor against neighbor.

And now, eighty years later, the same tactic is in wide and terrible use in our country. Right-wing media spews lies about gay people and other minorities, without being challenged by the FCC or any other entity to assure us that that media Is truthful. Outright lies have no place in legitimate news outlets.

Instead, some tell lies about transgender people in bathrooms, LGBTQ people grooming kids (whatever that means), children acting like cats as left-wing adults provide them with litter boxes at school, and kindergarteners taught about sex acts. ALL LIES.

I want to work to stop the lies, but I feel powerless. How do I reach people who listen to the lies of conservative pundits and politicians? This column certainly won't reach people who hear and believe the lies. If I were wealthy, I'd take ads on Fox NotNews, and entertainingly tell the truth. The Gay Agenda: breakfast, lunch, pickup dog poop, unsubscribe from a zillion emails, dinner, bedtime. No time for grooming (whatever that is).

But what do I do now?

By nightfall I had written to the *Rachel Maddow Blog* urging her to take on the issue of people listening only to opposing media and calling out those which lie. News should be reliably true. She'd do a great job with that.

Next, I wrote to *The Cape Gazette*.

> *Dear Editor,*
> *I love* The Cape Gazette *because it has readers of all political views, a rare thing these days. Today I hope that eyes other than in my political bubble read this.*
>
> *Five people died in a hate crime last week. None of them, or others who have been killed, were grooming*

anybody for anything, causing danger in restrooms, teaching kindergarteners about sex or any of the other outrageous lies found on conservative media or online hate speech. They were merely trying to live their lives, like the rest of us.

The shooters do the crimes but are pushed to violence by politicians and commentators demonizing minorities and making people fear them. Right from the Nazi playbook, the lies make good people turn on their neighbors.

Cling to your own political views about reproductive freedom, taxes, and policies, and I will cling to mine. But do not believe the lies spread by commentators and politicians gaining wealth and power by telling you to hate others.

Fay Jacobs
Rehoboth Beach

Hell, I don't know if it will be published or, if so, do a shred of good. But I had to do something. And I will try to do more to stop the lies. Stay tuned. I'm on a mission.

But simultaneously let's live *our* lives, joyously, as safely as possible, kindly and mindfully that if an occasion arises, we can dispel some of the demonizing lies.

JANUARY 2023

My Dance with Covid (or Farewell to 2022)

I'm a boomer party animal. I love to go out, eat, drink, enjoy live music, laugh with my friends, and age in place on a bar stool. Well, just like most everyone, Covid has screwed with my mojo.

And now it's New Year's Day 2023

I'm double vaccinated, triple boosted, and I hated wearing a mask until it was 13 degrees out and then I loved it.

Since 2020 I've stuck a special cotton swab up my nose so many times, I've dug a northwest passage directly to my hypothalamus. Sadly, that did not kill the spot regulating hunger.

Let me count the ways I shed my mask in the car and wound up crawling under the brake pedal, clawing for the hearing aid ejected with the mask.

At this writing, I have not yet had Covid, but it has tied me in gnarly knots anyway.

Last May, after quarantining prior to a vacation (postponed from 2020), I had supper with six friends who'd all tested negative that morning. The next day I got the dreaded phone call about a Typhoid Mary.

We spent a tortured ninety-six hours suspicious of every throat tickle and chomping Oreos to see if we could still taste. Yes, I could have tested with yogurt, but I'm me. Still checking for symptoms, I sniffed my entrée before sampling, seeking the true bouquet of the dry meatloaf. And it was the only time I was thankful to notice my dog passing gas.

We streamed video until our eyeballs changed sockets. Wait. Did I hear my mate cough? Is my headache from Covid or eight hours of *Tom Clancy's Jack Ryan* getting shot at ad nauseam? Wait! Do I feel nauseam?

Finally, on departure day, the car packed and hiking poles

ready, we tested for Covid. *No purple line. Negative. Saved!* Like uncaged animals, we flew to Utah to hike, climb, and take pictures at five Southwest National Parks.

Returning home mid-May, we spent the summer of 2022 with little Covid contact or worry. But come fall, my spouse needed a minor belly hernia repair (Climbing? Zipline? Hoisting a bag into the airplane overhead compartment?). So, it was back into ten-day presurgery Covid quarantine.

We paid for Netflix, Prime, Britbox, HBO, and Showtime. Once again refusing generous party invitations we were confined to home by the cozy Fire Stick. It's a pretty bleak existence when your only travel is to the porch to claim packages. How pathetic is it to be excited to go out just to have your nose professionally Roto-Rootered?

During my mate's postsurgical house arrest, we watched forty-two episodes of *Vera*, a British mystery requiring closed captions for our own language. We eventually had one joyous night out on the town before going right back into precautionary quarantine for an upcoming cruise (postponed from 2021).

While friends frolicked in the wild, we stayed housebound playing bitterly competitive board games, wondering if we'd actually make a forty-first anniversary. Paroled, we fled to our port of departure for what was a marvelous trip. Seeing the Acropolis was great, but we longed to celebrate the holiday season here at the beach.

Not a half hour after coming home, a pal we'd spent the entire week with aboard ship called to warn she'd tested freakin' positive. Auuggghhh!

Back in lockdown at Survivor Rehoboth, smelling, tasting, and testing to check our status, we watched British Bake-offs and the January 6 Committee show (most fascinating procedural on TV). We broke out after six days to socialize, eat, drink, and make merry, taking in the wonder of our hometown season.

That is, until December 15 and mandatory quarantine for

my December 22 knee surgery. When I sang "I'll be Home for Christmas," it was literal. And by the way, my torn meniscus was a souvenir from the Utah guidebook calling our final hike "fairly flat and quite easy." Liars!

But following surgery came my Christmas miracle. I felt well enough to hobble out for our traditional Jewish Christmas Eve at our favorite Chinese Restaurant. Then we donned our gay apparel to enjoy Christmas dinner with a large group of friends.

Our freedom lasted twelve hours. By morning we got word a dinner guest had flunked his Covid test. So much for frolicking for the last week of 2022. Jailbirds again, we got sprung in time to bump elbows with friends on New Year's Eve. Hell, midnight kisses are now extinct, and not touching somebody with a ten-foot pole is public health policy.

I'm still a Covid virgin. So, what if I only had twelve days of Christmas from Thanksgiving to New Years. The dance goes on.

FEBRUARY 2023

The Writer's Life

For a very good reason, life has gotten harder for writers. It's even more difficult, I think, for comic writers like me whose hallmark is familiar catch phrases and jokes based on common words.

That's because there's an ever-increasing list of words and phrases that are now to be avoided. Let me be clear, there is no formal list, and no punishments are handed down by editorial authorities. Although editors might delete them and if they stay, readers may call me out for using words that offend.

And that's the point. We are evolving to understand the origins of some common words and idioms, and even if we don't mean to offend, we do. It's a learning process.

One of my favorite lines in my comedy show used to be "My spirit animal is a rubber chicken." The audience laughed. But I've since been made aware that a spirit animal is a serious part of Native American religious culture. It's wrong and insensitive to make fun of it.

I've been thinking about using "My service animal is a rubber chicken." Is that offensive to people with disabilities? I'm not sure.

Likewise, at a writer's conference a few years ago, we called a session "Circling the Wagons" to mean coming together to tackle a problem. One of the Native-American members of the organization was upset.

None of us really ever thought about the origin of the phrase, or its connection to the widespread genocide of Native Americans. We changed the title. I just heard it on CNN the other day. But I won't use it anymore. Also, bye-bye to "off the reservation," which I no longer use to mean wildly off topic. I never meant to offend, but good intentions are no excuse for language I now know to be racist. So too "having a pow-wow," "low man on the totem pole," and "Indian giver." How the hell have we gotten to the twenty-first century not caring that these terms were insulting?

Did you know that calling something the "peanut gallery" does not refer to the 1950s *Howdy Doody Show* audience section? That phrase originated during segregation, when Black people were made to sit only in the balcony at movie theaters, and people made fun thinking they only ate peanuts. I had no idea. Now that I know its true meaning, it's dead to me.

Our country's shameful slaveholding past gave us a myriad of words and phrases we used without thinking of their original context. "Sold down the river," "Plantation," and even the phrase "Grandfathered in." Heck, that word is embedded in zoning and building codes all over America.

With dance floors not permitted in downtown Rehoboth, one large restaurant's dance floor was "grandfathered" to still exist. Nobody knew that the term was from the Reconstruction Era. If a Black man's grandfather voted, he could vote. I don't think that one is going to be expunged everywhere anytime soon, but I'm hesitant to use it.

Even in my comic zipline story I skirt trouble. I used the phrase "Zippity-Doo-Dah" from a song everyone knows from the film *Song of the South*. Now Disney has retooled one of its biggest attractions to remove that song. The film has long been out of circulation due to its being declared racist. I can substitute Zip, Zip and Away but the sound of the phrase is not as funny as using Doo-Dah.

I also don't know if we're going to stop calling Broadway chorus members gypsies anymore. Calling the nomadic Romani people, originally from Northern India and then Europe, Gypsies is derogatory to them. So too, the shortened verb "to gyp."

I hate to see our nomadic chorus kids, who go from show to

show, lose their designation. And I sure don't want to censor the title of one of my favorite Broadway musicals. But, like Whoopie Goldberg, who just got in hot water for using the term on TV's *The View*, I won't use the term gypped again.

I want it to disappear just as the pejorative and terribly hurtful phrase "Jew you down" has mostly gone from responsible writing. I've had it said in my presence, and it was super painful. Now that I'm aware where gypped comes from, it's out of my lexicon.

I was working on the script of the play Mike Gilles and I wrote about the Stonewall Inn. Yikes, every account describes young gay men being hauled off to jail in Paddy Wagons. That term hails from early New York and Boston when the immigrant Irish not only were the police drivers of the wagons but lots of Irishmen were frequently arrested for drunkenness. I'm sure there were all ethnicities in those police vehicles, but they were dubbed paddy wagons. Should I delete the term from quoted first-person accounts? I'm torn.

If I've missed any problematic words or phrases, I'm sure readers will alert me when they take offense. I promise to listen, and course correct as necessary. This writing life is tougher now, it's true, but it feels right to be more sensitive to others.

And what the hell, Artificial Intelligence will be doing my job by next week anyway. "Hey, ChatGBT, write something for me in the style of Fay Jacobs—oh, and watch out for slurs."

MARCH 2023

Paddling Against the Tide

I had the good fortune to be in Islamorada in the Keys this week. I was set to go paddling with veteran kayaker Sharon and my kayak-loving mate, Bonnie. As we schlepped Sharon's three heavy kayaks to the boat launch, I realized this part of the job was already enough exercise for me.

Anyway, I was already set to have a cardiac stress test the following week and figured I didn't need a rehearsal.

Nevertheless, cinched into life jackets, ready for a cruise ship muster station drill, we proceeded. I'd rather have been on Holland America to Cozumel.

Sharon's kayak was a fiberglass ultra-sleek racer, with a seat deep inside, clearly for the experienced paddler. Bonnie's boat was sleek but slightly wider for more stability and easier entry down into the craft.

My kayak looked like a floating Tupperware container. It was a vaguely oval big chunk of polyethylene plastic, which I was helped onto, to sit atop, not in.

"It's really stable," Sharon said, "not as easy to paddle as our skinny kayaks, but you'll be much safer and more comfortable."

Really?

The first two boats slid down the ramp into the bay. They were already two lengths ahead of me as I scooched my boat off the concrete and into the water using the paddle as a gondola pole. It immediately collapsed down to eighteen inches, and I was (here it comes) up the creek without a paddle. To be specific, Sharon and Bonnie were already up the creek, and I was still in the marina.

I used the mini paddle like I was in a canoe, switching from one side to the other, but finally found the button to enlarge it back into real kayak gear. At this point I started moving forward slowly, feeling fairly stable, at least physically.

Yes, paddling this floating food container wasn't that easy, but I soon fell into a decent rhythm, enjoying the sunshine and the ride. A large turtle surfaced, winking at me, and as seagulls swooped down, I apologized for not having any boardwalk fries.

We paddled for a long time with the wind picking up a bit and me bellowing happy show tunes in time to my paddling. Sharon was way out in front, Bonnie well behind her and, continually turning to make sure I was still bringing up the rear.

Suddenly the wind increased, shifted, and far away I saw Sharon turn and head back toward us. Bonnie stopped paddling and I kept going and we met in a three-boat huddle.

"Let's go back," Sharon said, "I'm seeing whitecaps and this much wind will make it tough."

Now I've been amid whitecaps before—from high up on the deck of a thrty-foot power boat. Whitecaps three inches from my eyeballs looked like a tsunami breaking over the bow of the S.S. Tupperware.

To say that paddling against the wind was difficult is like saying the Poseidon was a bathtub toy. Omigod, I was panting, gasping, and getting drenched. The show tunes turned to *Les Miserables*. With every stroke, I tried not to have one. I made wild animal noises, desperately seeking forward progress.

The swells came faster and higher now, meaning I could only point directly into the waves—a turn toward shore would have instantly swamped me. Dammit, my plan was to hang a right toward land and call an Uber.

With every two houses I passed, I was blown back one.

It took well over an hour and a half of ridiculously strenuous paddling before I saw our marina in the distance. Bon was way ahead of me, and Sharon was probably in the bar with a Mai Tai. When I finally got close to the ramp, I saw both of them waiting. Sharon's knees were bleeding. If *she* was injured dismounting, what hope did I have?

"You'll have to be careful," she hollered. "The ramp is slippery!"

Alas, as I grabbed Bonnie's hand to help me off, I slid on the slimy ramp, and landed, splayed flat out, on my back. Frantically trying to rise, I skidded further down the ramp, up to my belly button in the water. All I could do was lie there, laughing like a maniac. Thank goodness I was half submerged so nobody noticed me laughing so hard I peed.

"Are you okay???" Sharon exclaimed, not even waiting for my "Yes!!!" before continuing, "I was panicked. How could I do this to you? I was getting a friend to go out in his boat to rescue you when I saw Bonnie, and she said you were on the way. I was so worried."

I was still laughing like a lunatic. When I was finally hauled up, Bonnie said, "You did great. You had the hardest job paddling with that clunky kayak."

I know. And I'd paddled for hours without a single twinge in my chest. Of course, by morning I couldn't lift my right arm to brush my teeth. But I'm proud to have qualified for a Rubbermaid Kayak participation trophy.

Bring on the stress test. I've already aced it.

APRIL 2023

Juiced Up and Ready to Roll

I'm writing this while I'm still on an emotional high from Women's FEST. Although I'm not ruling out residual alcohol in my system.

Women's FEST was spectacular, and I give my thanks and accolades to everyone involved—committee, volunteers, staff, and CAMP Board members. What a blast!

I loved it all but was particularly thankful for the evening I spent performing at The Top of the Pines. I'll leave it to others, of course, to talk about the show, but I can tell you that for me, the venue, the audience, and the atmosphere was a joy. In my eight years of touring as a sit-down comic my night at the Pines is among my top feel-good experiences.

And lots of it has to do with drag queens. Individually and in general.

Individually, the great Kristina Kelly worked with me to set up and run tech, and the legendary Mona Lotts gave me a hilarious and heartfelt introduction. And they both welcomed me to their dressing room and their theatrical home.

And being there on stage allowed me to talk to my audience about drag queens in general—and how pissed off I am about desperate politicians going after our gorgeous, snarky queens to appease their bigot base. My audience agreed, with cheers for drag queens everywhere.

I adore our drag queens for lots of reasons, but especially because for all our success in fighting for our rights and LGBTQ equality, it was our drag queens helping to lead those efforts.

Drag queens and transgender women rioted in August 1966, three years before the Stonewall riots, at San Francisco's Compton's Cafeteria. Since cross-dressing and "impersonating" a woman were illegal at the time and transphobia kept transgender individuals out of most gay bars, many trans people and drag performers gathered at Compton's and were among the very first to fight—verbally and physically—for LGBTQ equality.

As for the legendary Stonewall Riots in 1969, drag queens and transgender women were instrumental in throwing the first rocks and punches there too.

And our drag queens were front and center at our first Pride Parades and influential in the success of our pioneering gay bars. I think so fondly about female impersonator Christopher Peterson performing in Rehoboth over the past quarter of a century. All of our talented local female impersonators. And the success of Billy Porter in *Pose* and RuPaul with his *Drag Race*. Drag queens are not only part of our LGBTQ culture, but they have also stepped well into the mainstream as RuPaul's fans will attest.

So, what the hell are these politicians doing picking on these wonderful artists and entertainers? It's my guess that Drag Queen Story hour was a positively brilliant idea to lure kids away from their video games or TikTok and into reading.

Last week, of all hideous things, packs of Neo-Nazis picketed and threatened performers at drag story hours at Ohio libraries and bookstores. Not only is the vision of a swastika flag flying in public horrifying, but this particular cluster of haters says that in 1940s Germany, Jews weren't the problem; gays were. I sputter to comment other than I'm frightened.

Tennessee just passed a drag law making it illegal for drag queens to perform for youngsters. In Florida a pending bill will enact large fines for venues that have drag performances where a child can spy them. Will they fine Pride organizations featuring drag queens on decorated floats tossing candy to families on parade routes?

In a country full of hideous problems, drag queens are what haters are obsessing over?

Given today's political realities, it's quite certain that MAGA mouthpieces started with drag queens and transgender youth but will soon come for the entire LGBTQ community when they need to widen their scope of hate. Look what they've already done to young women. Is Gay marriage next?

I am determined to hustle my aging ass back out on the streets to fight back. There's nothing like an angry old lesbian. I don't even care if I get arrested. You know me; nothing is so bad if it's worth the story you can tell.

I challenge all of us to get off our comfortable butts, cut down on TV streaming and get busy. Let's register voters, donate to the good guys, write letters, raise our voices, and make some good trouble! Who's in?

APRIL 2023

What Price Loyalty?

There's nothing like loyalty. But it can weigh you down.

I'm not talking about loyalty to family, friends, and country. That kind is uplifting.

But those ubiquitous loyalty programs every restaurant, grocery, airline, gas station, and credit card company dangles before us can get pretty heavy. Put those scannable loyalty tags on your key ring and you'll need a hula hoop.

When my keys got too heavy, I put the loyalty cards in my wallet, and it blew up like the Hindenburg. In fact, I was carrying so many punch cards, loyalty cards, and key tags I started to do something my family could never get this gay woman to do—carry a purse.

Loyalty is literally weighing me down, and I've got the vapors from weighing my purchasing choices. To be or not to be loyal is the question. And what price loyalty? Full price if you don't have a loyalty card.

Now this is really nothing new. Anybody remember collecting and using S&H Green Stamps in the 1960s? Yes, I'm that old. Actually, that program started in 1896, and no, I'm not *that* old. The S&H stamp craze struggled along until 1980.

The stamps worked the same way as today's rewards, being distributed at gas stations, department stores and groceries, but did not involve computers, passwords, pin numbers, or loyalty key tags. It was much simpler (as were the times, but that's a whole other column).

Lore has it that in the 1960s, S&H distributed more stamps than the postal service and distributed 35 million catalogues so collectors could buy breadboxes, ice trays, or shag rugs to go atop linoleum floors. You could even exchange them for that new Melmac dishware.

Contemporary loyalty programs work the same way, plus recording our visits and, according to industry experts, forging an emotional connection between brands and customers. I admit I get pretty emotional if I can't find my loyalty card and cause a backup at a cash register. I get extra emotional if I wind up having to pay the same price as disloyal folks.

I'm also convinced that the Tuesday free coffee perk for Wawa loyalists leads to more exorbitant prices on the rest of what's perking there. But I dutifully jump from bed Tuesday mornings to get my free coffee rather than suffer the guilt from ignoring a freebie. This particular emotional connection borders on a diagnosis.

According to marketing gurus, loyalty programs change our behavior, just as they were designed to do. They dictate where we shop, eat, gas up, send packages from, the whole gamut. Consumers are statistically 25 percent more likely to spend money at a business where we have taken a loyalty oath. I'd rather find a place which encourages me to pay 25 percent less.

Earning rewards on a credit card is particularly insidious. I now charge all my retail and restaurant purchases to my rewards card. I even assign my monthly bills to the credit card.

Of course, I gave myself a strict ultimatum, vowing I'd immediately transfer cash from my checking account to my credit card to cover every single purchase or bill I've paid on credit. Oh, puleeze. Now my rewards are diluted by credit card interest. I've got an emotional connection all right; I'm pissed I'm going to debtor's prison.

I could really use some time away on a cruise ship for an entire week free from the pressure to shop and dine only with businesses with whom I have sworn loyalty.

And I'd get more points on my credit card paying for the cruise while simultaneously adding loyalty points with the cruise company. By this time, I'm either a Commodore, Boatswain, or Barnacle with one cruise company. I have a chest so full of loyalty medals I could stand in for a rear admiral.

So, what's a consumer to do? Be happy with the discounts, perks and rewards of modern marketing I suppose and ignore the incessant pressure to be loyal.

Although it was fun during that 13-degree cold snap last Christmas to use my grocery loyalty card to scrape ice off my windshield. I got about 10 percent off.

MAY 2023

Reflections from Kodak

Not only am I aging gracelessly, but I just watched myself do it. I've just completed digitizing my photographs from 1965 to 1980. I did this by removing them from deteriorating, disintegrating scrapbooks and albums and scanning the fading photos into my computer. Then, I preserved them, improved them, and curated out the people I no longer wished to remember. My ex-husband the accordion player (vintage '73-'78) now makes only a brief guest appearance.

It's astonishing how the once bright, colorful four-by-sixes of Disney World, Chesapeake Bay, or even Paris had turned to a brownish-sepia. Luckily my memories of good experiences, fun theater productions, and dear friends are still bright in my mind.

But the pictures did tell me a very clear, visible, wistful story. Before I came out to myself and others in early 1980, my life was indeed sepia-toned. Not bright. Not authentic. Not happy.

Yes, I loved my college and theater friends. And escaping into theater saved me, as it has done for many gay youngsters, afraid, closeted or in denial. But truly, in those early photographs, from high school on, I saw my unhappiness and my longing for a more authentic life. I saw it on my face, in my posture, in my clothing. It's uncanny. I tried so hard to be straight I even straightened my curly hair.

So, I stopped scanning the pictures at the day before I stepped from the closet. Those hundreds of pictures now digitally preserved will be printed in a pre-coming-out album I just ordered from an online photo company. This album will take up a tiny fraction of the bookshelf space where those big, fat, fading, falling apart scrapbooks used to stand. And I'll have saved my old sepia life.

So next up I'll scan the happier photos of myself. I'm still marveling over the distinctly visible change in my smile, my appearance, and my whole persona before and after coming out. I was hiding in plain sight.

And this revelation makes me think of Florida and other states where *Don't Say Gay* is taking hold and LGBTQ people are being harassed, hated, or targeted simply for who they are.

I worry about youngsters having a much harder time coming out in this new era of hate.

I worry about the ugly choices parents might have to make in order to get their trans youngsters health care.

I worry about my transgender friends in states that might outlaw their access to hormone therapy.

I worry about young people, out since their teens, who have never faced much discrimination. How will they handle it?

I worry about my friends in Florida and other states being turned away from health care because they are gay. The Supreme Court just allowed that kind of discrimination. I already know of two friends whose primary care doctors felt a need to assure them it would not happen at that particular medical practice. But it surely will happen at others.

You know what I *don't* worry about? I do not worry that LGBTQ people will stop coming out, that they will stay in sepia-toned lives rather than living in full-spectrum color. We are nothing if not colorful. We are the rainbow. And we're here, we're queer, and we vote.

JUNE 2023

Enjoy Yourself, it's Earlier Than You Think

I just gave a bag of random glassware to Goodwill, including some bar glasses with the words Geezer, Coot, and Fogey etched on them. They were probably a gag gift for my fiftieth birthday.

Now, a quarter century later, I'd rather gag than serve drinks in those glasses to my guests. Heck, people may have come to happy hour directly from physical therapy, a stress test or colonoscopy. These days I run into more of my friends waiting to have blood drawn than at our favorite watering hole.

But on the plus side, we're mostly in good shape. I'm not wearing the orthopedic shoes and housecoats (do they still exist?) my grandmothers wore in their fifties. Their early fifties!

Is it just me, or does this decade seem younger now than when we thought of it at ages twenty-five or fifty? So many of my friends in their seventies are out kayaking, hiking, playing pickleball, and whooping it up in ways unthinkable to my ancestors.

In fact, at my stepmother Joan's independent living facility (she's an active ninety-three), we were told that a decade ago the median age for people moving into the facility was seventy-six. These days, it's eighty-six. See? At our ages we *are* younger-acting than previous generations were at this same milestone.

Of course, this does not make up for the sting we suffer when we visit "the home" and everybody in the elevator asks us "Moving in?"

No, not yet. With role models like Jane Fonda, Lily Tomlin, Rita Moreno and Sally Field, those of us on either side of three-quarters of a century are being as brazen and active as those celebrities. Albeit with fewer facelifts, baggier eyes, and more wobbly jowls.

By contrast, I have a photo of my grandparents on their fortieth anniversary. They stand with ramrod posture behind a cake, grandma wearing a sedate black dress, grandpa in a dark suit and tie. They are not quite smiling. It could double for mug shots.

In a polar opposite, our fortieth anniversary photo has us in T-shirts (mine said "I'm Not Old, I'm Mid-Century Modern), grinning like Cheshire cats, drinking giant martinis, and surrounded by friends and gorgeous drag queens.

We do, of course, make some concessions to age. I kayak with gusto, but when getting in or out of the vessel it takes a village. Likewise, I find happy hour dining (I refuse to call it the early bird special) more suitable than dinner at eight.

Last winter in Florida, after evening boating, we returned to the dock at extreme low tide. The pier towered five feet above us. The young athletic captain and his companion got off the boat with some embarrassing difficulty. Not being ninja warriors, our only hope was a helicopter to pluck us off the ship.

"We're sleeping on the boat." I told the captain. He smiled.

"Go for it," he said, "High tide is 7:15 a.m."

We bid them adieu, turned up the music and air conditioning, opened a bottle of vino, enjoyed a nightcap and slept like babies. Waking at 7, we had coffee and stepped up about two inches to walk right off the boat onto the pier. Now that was an enjoyable age-related accommodation.

Likewise, while partying with friends (some much younger) we keep up really well with the dining, drinking, and entertainment. Sometimes age is a plus. When standing next to a thumping audio speaker I can dull the pain by turning off my hearing aids. Ahhhh ...

And, at a certain point, like 10 p.m., we've learned it's fine to pull the ripcord, order an Uber and say" See you tomorrow."

Frankly, instead of being completely appalled at approaching the three-quarter-century mark, I'm thankful to be surrounded by friends, fun, and enriching experiences. While I'm in better shape than the vision I had of myself as a seventy-five-year-old, I admit, it hurts a little putting it in print.

But I was buoyed by the words of my ninety-five-year-old cousin whom I get to see once a year. I was paying our lunch check when she said, "Okay, but my treat next year." Now *that's* confidence. I hope she gets the chance to pick up the tab in 2024 and I hope I'm as lucky as she is in my aging process.

In the meantime, may I get timely Ubers, take all those tests but have no bad results, and remember to turn my hearing aids back on after the music dies. After all, I'd hate to miss the server asking if I want another dirty martini.

JUNE 2023

Civility Lives!

On May 18 I went to a meaningful event at the University of Delaware where a Civility in Public Service Award was bestowed. Civility. That's something we sure could use more of these days.

And to be in the room for this event, representing CAMP along with CAMP Rehoboth Vice-President Leslie Ledogar was rewarding on its own. To be there with our two U.S Senators, Tom Carper and Chris Coons, plus the two senators being honored and a room full of attendees was indeed a privilege.

The award, from the UD's Biden School of Public Policy and Administration, went to U S Senator Tammy Baldwin and US Senator Susan Collins. Baldwin, an out and proud gay woman representing Wisconsin, is a Democrat, and Collins, a longtime senator from Maine, is a Republican.

That they were honored for sponsoring and ushering through Congress (no easy task) the Respect for Marriage Act codifying both Gay and interracial marriage is clearly an act of bipartisan civility. Bravo to them.

Their efforts sprang to action right after the Supreme Court vacated Roe v. Wade giving states the right to rule on abortion however they wished. The court had nullified its own 1973 ruling on the national right to abortion.

They could do so since the court's fifty-year-old ruling legalizing abortion country-wide had never been codified (put into law) by Congress. In the half century since the ruling, no one got a bill passed by Congress writing the legalization of abortion into US law. They trusted the Supremes not to reverse what they called "settled law." Oops.

Fearful that the Supreme Court's 2015 legalization of gay

marriage could crash the exact same way, Baldwin and Collins sponsored the Respect for Marriage Act. They wrote the law to include codification of both gay and interracial marriage (that having been "settled" by the Supreme Court in 1967) and away they went trying to get it passed in Congress.

I have to say, I have often disagreed with positions Senator Collins has taken, most recently, her confidence that the Supreme Court would not tinker with settled law on the Roe v. Wade decision.

But to her credit, when they disappointed her by overturning the abortion ruling, she actually did something about it. She and Baldwin sponsored the Respect for Marriage Act and against formidable odds got the law passed.

Both she and Senator Baldwin spoke about how they won this one. "We listened," said Collins, "asking senators what they needed to vote yes." When some said, "assurances religious institutions would not be forced to conduct marriages against their tenets," the authors wrote those protections into the bill. Some opposed the bill because they thought it would legalize polygamy or other practices, said Baldwin. Again, they went one by one for the votes they needed and answered their colleague's specific questions. It was grassroots politics at the highest level, with the senators and their allies working the phones, walking the halls of Congress, and securing the votes they needed.

Senator Collins told of a moment on Thanksgiving Day, just as she was basting the big bird, when a phone call from Baldwin presented a problem. Luckily the two senators worked out a solution well before the sweet potatoes could get cold.

"We never gave up," Collins said, finally coming up with twelve Republican votes and passage of the bill.

"And we were able to repeal that ugly Defense of Marriage Act" from the Clinton era, Baldwin said.

Collins and Baldwin were two generals from opposite sides who used civility and great political skills to get the Respect for

Marriage Act passed—something that may prove invaluable to the LGBTQ and interracial marriage community in the future.

Thankfully, Gay marriage is now protected, the senators were lauded for civility, and we go on from here.

But to where? We all know there has been increasing incivility, anti-trans and LGBTQ hatred in state legislatures, on the streets, and all-over social media. I myself just heard about a comment made on a local golf course. "I don't mind homosexuals. I just don't want them to flaunt it."

Flaunt it? What is this, 1987? What does that ancient comment even mean anymore? If it means I can't talk about my wife and schnauzer when you talk about your husband and collie, we are in deep poop. If that line is making a comeback in anti-gay rhetoric, we are all on notice.

If we must, we're all going to celebrate Pride Month (thank you City of Rehoboth for proclaiming it so) and then get back in the trenches, win people over one by one, and bring back all manner of civility. On your mark, get set . . .

JUNE 2023

Downhill from Here

A quarter of a century ago we took a birthday trip with friends to Paris. The one in France. My pal Larry and I were turning fifty within a month of each other. We checked into a small Left Bank hotel on the day of his birthday, followed by a three-hour gourmet experience at a restaurant in the shadow of the Eiffel Tower. *Magnifique!*

The next morning Larry sought Coca Cola and Imodium after reporting a horrid night, resplendent with all manner of *mal d'estomac.* "I knew things would start to go downhill after turning fifty, but I didn't think it would happen this fast," he sputtered. We've laughed about this for twenty-five years.

Well, on the very cusp of my having the next quarter century birthday, I got sick. It probably started as a pulmonary reaction to my being an idiot. I went boating on the day last June when smoke and pollution from the Canadian wildfires infested our area skies. The next day my spouse compounded the idiocy by refusing to give up a tee time. Did I sit out eighteen holes with air conditioning? Of course not. I went to a farmers market, relaxed in my hot tub, and otherwise inhaled the lung-poisoning smoke plus the added benefit of Route One bumper-to-bumper tailpipe emissions.

And on the third day they went to an outdoor concert where they may or may not have come in contact with any number of co-morbidity disease germs. The concert was fantastic, we were morons.

And on the seventh day they both had pneumonia. Seriously.

What followed was almost three weeks spent in the house together. Sick as proverbial dogs, neither of us could muster the energy to cook, do laundry, pay bills, let the dog out, let the dog in, get the mail, or do anything but cough, wheeze, and eat Oreos. We often resorted to Rock Paper Scissors to allocate jobs. The house became Hoarders Are Us.

While amazingly no writs of divorce were filed, we survived nine prescriptions filled, eight Chinese or Italian food deliveries, four urgent care visits (they do chest x-rays), three medicines paid out-of-pocket because crème-de-la-crème insurance refused to cover them, two primary care visits, and a huge debt to Door Dash.

This was followed by weeks and weeks of continued coughing by both of us. Then I had an asthma attack—something I have not had for thirty-five years. Bonnie recovered completely, but I am still dealing with a pulmonologist. The doctor thinks we both had the new virus RSV, for which, now that the horses got out of the corral, I am now vaccinated against.

While I still refuse to act my age, my body seems to have another agenda. I knew that when I turned seventy-five things would start to go downhill, but I had no idea it would happen this fast. Stayed tuned for medical updates. I'm rethinking my motto that nothing is so bad if it's worth the story you can tell.

JULY 2023

Get Off of My Lawn!

As a mid-century modern gal, I have developed an intolerance for stupidity, bad customer service and the outrageous behavior we currently see all around us.

Traveling I-95 recently, two muscle cars zoomed past, weaving in and out, racing like lunatics, narrowly missing bumper after bumper.

"What's the matter with people?" I groused for the hundredth time this week.

Then came three motorcycles driving at ridiculous speeds, zigzagging between lanes, frightening drivers, and missing rearview mirrors by inches. I half-expected to see these Evil Evel Knievelites splattered on the road up ahead.

"Morons!" I shouted.

We arrived at our Geek Squad appointment where a sullen, fledgling adult in a man bun grunted hello and was clearly impatient with our questions. He said we were stupid for keeping a phone for more than two years. He stared at my spouse's iPhone 7 as if it was a pink Princess Phone.

After grudgingly fixing the antique, this tech wunderkind took our $40 in cash, glaring at it as if we'd paid in pirate doubloons. Mumbling "Bye," he returned to his iPad game like we'd interrupted his day.

"What's the matter with . . ."

To soothe our wounded egos, we stopped for a fancy coffee. I stood at the counter along with absolutely no other customers and waited for somebody to notice me. Two employees ambled back and forth several times in front of me, talking to each other but not saying a word to me. What am I, on the TV show *Ghosts*? I get that the workers might have been legitimately busy, but a smile and "I'll be with you in a minute" would kill them?

When a person finally showed up to the cash register, she just stood, stone-faced, waiting for me to speak. I got the hint and ordered. "That it?" she mumbled. And two minutes later she returned and simply pointed to the other side of the counter. I got that charade clue too and grabbed my drinks.

"What's the . . ."

Back in the car we sipped our caramel mocha macchiato chai whatevers, repeating our disbelief at the treatment we'd received and the invisibility we were accorded. "What's the matter with people?"

Then it hit me. That's it. We'd now become the female versions of those two cranky old Muppets in the balcony from *The Muppet Show*—cantankerous geezers who grouse at everything.

While I'm not shouting, "Get off My Lawn!" like Clint Eastwood's famous grumpy old man (unless it's with your pooping dog and you don't clean up), I now identify full-time as one of those complaining old-coot puppets.

So yesterday, after watching news of the latest mass shooting ("What's the *matter* with people?"), being on hold with the cable company long enough to train a puppy, ("What's the matter . . ."), and dealing with a contractor who said he'd be at my house Wednesday, but apparently declined to specify *which* Wednesday ("What's the . . ."), I had had it.

"Let's get in the hot tub and try to relax," my spouse suggested, coming out of the bedroom in only her robe.

"I'd love that," I said, "but it's still daylight out. You know I won't go in until dark without my bathing suit."

Whereupon my mate explained to me, for the zillionth time, that no windows overlook our yard, nobody can see over our fence, and I was silly being so modest in our own private oasis.

I held my ground, went to put my suit on, and so did she, although her frustration clearly showed. We got into the tub, turned on the bubbler, sipped our happy hour cocktails, and truly relaxed.

And then we heard it. "Hi," said a very young voice. We looked up to see a girl, maybe seven or eight years old, perched in a tree overlooking our six-foot fence.

"Hi," she repeated, waving.

Well, we weren't invisible. Our tree-climber was friendly, not grunting at us, not staring at any electronic device, and sat perched in the tree like the character Scout in *To Kill a Mockingbird* might have done.

We waved back, shouted "Hi," and as she scampered down and ran away giggling, we started laughing and could not stop. I turned the noisy bubbler up so our maniacal laughter wouldn't alert any nearby mental health professionals.

I was so glad I won the bathing suit argument. For our dignity's sake, and most certainly for her sensitive eyes, I'm happy we wrinkled boomers weren't buck naked.

But oddly, this whole episode gave me hope. Not that I encourage a new generation of Peeping Toms, but maybe, when our tree-climbing friend grows up to an after-school job, she'll reform customer service to its friendly past, by saying "Hi," and treating her elders like people.

I can dream, can't I?

JULY 2023

A Trivial Pursuit

One night recently we made a humiliating attempt at several contemporary versions of the game Trivial Pursuit. We were unable to answer any music questions about genres newer than the '90s, couldn't answer Silver Screen questions about famous film editors, or have any luck at all with the Millennium edition. So, I took my baby boomer self to a thrift store and found the original 1980 Genus classic version of the game.

Like an old friend, the game gave our geezer quartet a delightful evening of the familiar—with only a few mitigating factors. For one thing, some of the 1980 questions had, well, expired.

What is the name of the principal governing committee of the USSR?

I answered "defunct." But to win I had to say Politburo. Never mind that there is no Union of Soviet Socialist Republics and hasn't been since George H.W. Bush was president.

Who assassinated Robert F. Kennedy and when will he first be eligible for parole?

Parole????? We knew the assassin was Sirhan Sirhan, but according to the game, the correct answer had him being eligible for parole in 1994. Okay, that's terrifying. "My God, is he out among us?" somebody asked. Thanks to the Google machine, we toasted to the fact that he was denied parole umpty-ump times, most recently last March. He's seventy-nine and still aging gracelessly in the clink.

Naturally, many of the science and geography questions had answers that remained the same more than forty years later. We knew lots of the entertainment answers too, but those pesky history questions kept us on our toes.

Whose courtship was considered the love story of the century?

Which century??? Turns out either way it was royal, as the twentieth century answer was Wallis Simpson and Edward VIII while we voted that the twenty-first century lovers were Meghan and Spare Heir Harry. We then digressed into a discussion of the rumors of their current split, finally deciding we didn't care.

After refilling our wine glasses, we continued to try to come up with correct answers to no longer relevant inquiries.

Who was the oldest US president elected?

Ha! Not Ronald Reagan anymore. It's Delaware's own Joe!

Who was the youngest golfer to win the Masters? In 1980 it was twenty-three-year-old Spaniard Severino Ballesteros. Incorrect now, thanks to Tiger Woods, who, when he won, was barely at legal drinking age.

What country contains the medieval seaport of Dubrovnik? Well, the game wanted us to answer Yugoslavia, but that country is completely gone, and that gorgeous city is now in Croatia.

And we completely ignored any geography questions concerning the African continent as we did not want our heads to explode.

At one point, an especially aggressive roll of the die sent the spotted cube hurtling off the table and onto the floor beneath my chair. There was a stunned moment of silence followed by a burst of laughter when we realized that one of our gracelessly aging quartet would have to navigate off a chair, squat down under the table, and retrieve the thing. And try to get up again.

"Delay of Game," I yelled. Wow, I used to drop something and automatically pick it up. Now when I drop something, I wonder if I still need it. So, we got the hint and gave up playing the actual game. Without the lost die we continued drinking wine and answering the questions, laughing at the number of queries that had become extinct.

But I have to admit, even some of the still-correct questions stumped us.

What's Howdy Doody's sister's name? It's Heidi Doody if you care.

What does a CBer refer to as a pregnant roller skate? Not only didn't we know the answer, but we also couldn't figure out the question. What's a CBer (Seeber?) . . . oh! C-B-er. Citizen's Band radio. We'd forgotten about that fad. "Breaker 1-9 Good Buddy—" Oh, and the answer is: a Volkswagen.

Here are a few boomer-era goodies for you.

1) *What's Radar O'Reilly's favorite drink?*
2) *Who portrayed Mrs. Robinson in The Graduate?*
3) *What were TV's Doreen Tracy, Cheryl Holdridge and Cubby O'Brien?* (see answers below)

And by the way, when we got to the question *How many dots are there on a pair of dice?* we knew it was time to for one of us to crawl under the table and retrieve the errant die. No boomers were injured in the making of this fine evening's fun.

Answers
(1) Grape Nehi
(2) Anne Bancroft
(3) Mouseketeers

AUGUST 2023

Size Matters

We rented a small camper for an entire month of glamping (glamor camping), boating, and relaxing) along beautiful Lake Champlain in Vermont. The minute we arrived; we knew we were doomed.

The tiny Retro camper was cute, but *waaaay* smaller than we saw online. But it was our bad. We googled the 19-foot model unaware the company also made a 15-footer—not online. Our lodging was 15 by 6 feet, or ninety square feet.

How small was it? When we tossed the dog inside, he wondered why he was back in crate training.

How small was it? You had to go outside to change your mind.

How small was it? It had twin beds on either side with a fridge and a toilet between the sleeping shelves. Opposite was a microwave and sink. Even skinny people couldn't squeeze past each other.

About the potty. If you sat and closed the door, you kneecapped yourself. Bending over for toilet paper risked traumatic brain injury. Going to pee? Wear a bike helmet. It was not a bathroom; it was an isolation booth. And by no means was it the cone of silence.

Relieving myself, I quickly discovered I had to stand up, step outside, do the Hokey Pokey and turn myself around to go back in to use the foot pedal pump out. We had a hand-held shower, but why? If I sat and sprayed myself, I'd break an elbow. I'd need roller derby protection.

It didn't matter, though. Turns out the hot water heater was dead.

We moved into the confined space and learned a violent

storm was forecast, including a possible tornado. Thunder, lightning, and torrential rain pounded the tin roof for hours. One leak and we'd be in a front-loading washing machine. One tornado gust and we'd be airborne. Mercifully, we stayed in our bunks, remained watertight, and survived Night One.

By Day Two I realized there was no mirror in the rig, which was just as well. Luckily the electric worked for my Keurig. It was overcast that morning, but we sat outside in our camp chairs, reading, and taking in the stunning lake view.

In Day Three's rain we joined friends at the Von Trapp Family Brewery, where Do, Re, Me had beer and enjoyed the hot water in the spacious Von Trapp Family Bathrooms. You could hide a whole children's singing group from the Nazis in there.

Later in the week the sun appeared so we enjoyed a terrific pontoon adventure on the lake. Glorious! Returning for happy hour, I tried a hammock stretched pretty high between two trees. Pretty high myself, I pulled the hammock edge under my butt, twisted slightly, raised one leg, and flipped myself tits down into a mud puddle. It took two spotters to get me back into the hammock. The eventual dismount took a village.

By Week Two our Barbie camper turned terrarium. Escaping mildew, we visited several superb restaurants, saw a movie, sat in our crate reading, and visited friends' places for showers and home-cooked food. Back at the tin can, we did have happy hours, despite scant room to shake a martini.

Aha! Sunrise with actual sun. We walked the kayaks from our site to the steps down to the lake. As we positioned the second kayak atop the steps, the weight of the vessel shifted, and momentum sent the thing sliding all the way down the steps and shooting into the lake headed for Canada.

Screaming ensued, as Bonnie jumped in the remaining kayak and went to rescue the runaway rental. Frankly, I was already calculating replacement cost. But she got it back. We went kayaking and another of our planned activities came to fruition.

By the beginning of the third week in the sardine can, the dog started to crack. Windsor was tired of having to choose which twin bed to sleep in. This wasn't glamping or even camping; it was Survivor Vermont. Ah the aroma of Deep Woods Off! in the morning.

Then, on Facebook we spied friends betting on how long we'd last. I was humbled by those wagering we'd make the full thirty-one-day stretch and likewise distracted by folks calling us home and wondering why I'd agreed to this foolishness in the first place.

When the Weather Channel forecast another whole week of dreary weather, we knew our party of three could not survive more micro house arrest. We made it to Day Twenty-One before pulling the rip cord.

"Congrats," said a pal, "Twenty-one days wins the championship on the reality show *Naked and Afraid*."

Heck, I'll take the trophy. We did abandon all clothes to bathe and shampoo in Lake Champlain. We were naked and the boaters buzzing by were probably afraid.

Heading south, we raced to get back to Rehoboth and our ginormous Taj Ma Manufactured Mansion. We loved Lake Champlain and loved spending time with friends, but now tiny houses are dead to me. Camping is dead to me. It's possible that vacationing is dead to me. But I did win *Naked and Afraid*.

SEPTEMBER 2023

Epilogue

I'm writing this in September 2023, a whole year before a national election, and we are already inundated with campaign ads, donation requests, and 24/7 news about polls, felonies, trials, appeals, and the stunning corruption of Trump World. By the time you're reading this, the frenzy will have accelerated to insane levels.

I don't have to tell you how appalled I am at the newly invigorated hatred coming at LGBT folks, especially the attacks on transgender youth and the help they need. The increased racism makes me sick. The bizarre attack on drag queens makes me incredulous. WTF is wrong with the MAGAs?

Please somebody send one of my books to Ron DeSantis so he can ban me. I'd love that badge of honor. And, from what I hear, I'll get an enormous jump in sales. The hell with Don't Say Gay, I want him to say Don't Say Fay!

Will the Supreme Court continue to set us back a half a century? Will democracy endure in this country? Will anti-LGBTQ+ forces prevail? Will we ever get rid of that alphabetical tongue twister LGBTQ+ with a better label?

As I close this last book of mine, I only have two more thoughts I would like to share. First, I really still believe that nothing is so bad if it's worth the story you can tell. And second, this is our circus. These are our monkeys. Please vote to preserve democracy.

ACKNOWLEDGMENTS

Usually, this page is to thank folks who helped get this book to readers. Instead, I'm talking about the folks who helped get all six of my books to readers, gave me a whole new midlife career in humor-writing and advocacy, and even launched me into a retirement gig in sit-down comedy.

Absolutely none of this would have happened without the late CAMP Rehoboth Executive Director and *Letters from CAMP* editor Steve Elkins. He gave me ink in 1995 (digital came later) with which to have a voice. He remains my hero.

Next came the very dear late publishers Anyda Marchant and Muriel Crawford, of A&M Books, who published my first book, a collection of my columns, in 2004. Anyda and Muriel, a couple for 57 years, were two of the founders of the legendary Naiad Press. Rehoboth's Gertrude Stein and Alice B. Toklas, they represented over half a century in the evolution of lesbian literature in America. I was lucky enough to know them, love them, learn from them and agree to try, to the best of my ability, to carry on for them with A&M Books.

Following that first book came an invitation from *Delaware Beach Life* magazine publisher Terry Plowman to contribute the column "Flotsam and Jetsam" to his publication. He assigned brilliant cartoonist Rob Waters to illustrate the columns—they made me howl and made readers laugh. Three of my books included *Delaware Beach Life* columns along with those published in *Letters*. Terry, thank you for including me and reminding me of deadlines.

Finally, enormous thanks to Salem West and Ann McMan of Bywater Books, which carried on the work of A&M Books and published my fifth and now sixth and final book in the Frying Series. Ann McMan's brilliant book covers and Salem West's nurturing as publisher are precious to me, as is their friendship. Thank you for keeping me in print and fried chicken.

Now I'm trying my best to retire, but it eludes me. Marj Shannon is the new *Letters* editor, and she invites me to write a column or feature or two when the spirit moves me. Thanks, Marge. *Letters* is lucky to have such a wonderful editor. And so am I.

And to Terry Plowman, thanks again for the privilege of still being in the pages of *Delaware Beach Life*. I must continue to have fun adventures so I can come up with columns for you. It's good for me.

But finally, to my readers. Steve Elkins once said that taken as a whole, aside from the humor, the Frying Series is a history of gay rights in America during the last quarter century. I'm proud of that. And of all the fun things I've written about as well. It's been decades of progress and good times. Let's beat back the dark and hope fun and progress continues.

Thanks for reading. Love you all.

ABOUT THE AUTHOR

Fay Jacobs, a native New Yorker, spent 30 years in the Washington, DC area working in journalism, theater, and public relations. She's a humorist, storyteller, and LGBTQ activist. Her first book, *As I Lay Frying: a Rehoboth Beach Memoir* was published in 2004. Since then, she has published *Fried & True: Tales from Rehoboth*; *For Frying Out Loud: Rehoboth Beach Diaries*; *Time Fries: Aging Gracelessly in Rehoboth Beach*; and *Fried & Convicted: Rehoboth Beach Uncorked*.

She has contributed feature stories and columns to such publications as *The Washington Post*, *The Advocate*, *OutTraveler*, *Curve Magazine*, *The Baltimore Sun*, *Chesapeake Bay Magazine*, *The Washington Blade*, *The Wilmington News Journal*, and more.

Since 1995 she has been a regular columnist for *Letters from CAMP Rehoboth*, and since 2010 she has had a monthly column in the award-winning *Delaware Beach Life Magazine*.

Since 2015, Fay has been touring with her one-woman show, *Aging Gracelessly: 50 Shades of Fay*.

She and Bonnie, her partner of 42 years and wife of 12 years, are aging in place on the beach or on bar stools in Rehoboth Beach, Delaware with their spoiled schnauzer, Windsor. Fay is thrilled to have found a home at Bywater Books.

Bywater Books believes that all people have the right to read or not read what they want—and that we are all entitled to make those choices ourselves. But to ensure these freedoms, books and information must remain accessible. Any effort to eliminate or restrict these rights stands in opposition to freedom of choice.

Please join with us by opposing book bans and censorship of the LGBTQ+ and BIPOC communities.

At Bywater Books, we are all stories.

We are committed to bringing the best of contemporary literature to an expanding community of readers. Our editorial team is dedicated to finding and developing outstanding writers who create books you won't want to put down.

For more information about Bywater Books, our authors, and our titles, please visit our website.

https.bywaterbooks.com

www.ingramcontent.com/pod-product-compliance
Lightning Source LLC
Chambersburg PA
CBHW060515080526
44586CB00012B/493